Perhaps you've
(TCK) or a "miss
riences will make you feel what it's like for so many kids growing up between vastly different cultures. Far from being a bitter story, this is a sweet one of growing up in a family given to following God's will across the sea, and with that growth, learning to make that same faith her own.

—Joy Anglea, MD

Faith has a wonderfully evocative writing style, using words to paint vivid pictures of life in Hong Kong and China through the eyes of a child, teenager, and young adult. While this writing project was spurred on by her desire to integrate the seemingly disparate aspects of her life in various places around the globe, the reader is provided with a glimpse of how God can weave even such unraveled strands together into a beautiful tapestry of His making. As I read Faith's story, I found myself reflecting on how God has worked in my own life, using unexpected and sometimes difficult circumstances, and relationships with particular people to open up new possibilities and lead me in directions I would not have foreseen.

—Heather Davediuk Gingrich, PhD
Author of *Restoring the Shattered Self: A Christian Counselor's Guide to Complex Trauma*

A descriptive memoir of one young girl growing up in two cultures. The book provides a glimpse, only a glimpse, of the challenges and blessings of "becoming" when merging the realities of two cultures that do not intersect easily. What all third culture kids experience, Faith is able to articulate well through the writing of her childhood to adulthood experience.

—Cathy Hall- former missionary
Author of *God's Love Letters to Me: A Journey Through Loss and Grief*

I had a layover in Hong Kong once; reading *Unraveled* felt like an invitation to return to Hong Kong and stay a while. This captivating story is a look at the mission field through the eyes of a missionary kid, those often misunderstood third-culture kids who don't quite seem to "fit in" anywhere. As Faith shares her journey, she ultimately finds her sense of belonging in her identity in Christ, a place we all must come to regardless of the culture we identify with. Faith's book will stir you to set the compass of your heart to the true north that is found in Jesus alone.

—Michelle Elaine Burton
Author of *Seasons of Change* and
Losing Yourself and Finding Joy

I felt like I was taking Faith's hand as we ventured together through her life journey. We started down a road seeing things from a child's eyes. Her life turned from the stable, secure and familiar to the unknown as she became aware of the adventures of being in a missionary family. As a small child she would look up into the faces of adults who would influence and shape her life. She would look up at the skyscrapers all around her in an unfamiliar environment. Her life path would sometimes take her from wonderment and awe to despair and disappointment yet the Lord sustained her. I enjoyed taking the journey with her through the pages of her book!

—Gayle Tomlinson
Missionary wife with Barnabas 1040.com

Unraveled

a memoir

faith dea

To Bro. Ted and Sister Lynn with much love and appreciation,
Stephanie Dillon
I Sam. 25:13, 30:24

Unraveled

© 2024 Faith Dea
Colorado Springs, CO 80930

All rights reserved. Printed in the United States of America. No part of this publication may be mechanical, photocopying, recording or otherwise, without the written permission of the publisher.

Some people's names and certain details of their stories have been changed or modified to protect the privacy of the individuals involved. However, the facts of what happened surrounding the events described in this book have been conveyed as accurately as possible.

The use of material from or references to various websites does not imply endorsement of those sites in their entirety.

Cover & interior design by Typewriter Creative Co.

ISBN 979-8-9898240-0-7 (Paperback)
ISBN 979-8-9898240-1-4 (eBook)

*To mom and dad,
the road you took became my road to writing this book.
My story is possible because of you.*

*And to my husband and children,
for unwittingly adding inspiration for this journey.*

Contents

Prologue 9
Kai Tak 13
Baucum Beginnings 21
The Upstairs Window 31
Church 39
Beacon Hill 49
Baby Sister 57
Dear Friends 65
Mum 73
New Territories 81
Butterfly Bay 89
Texas 97
Deeper Waters 107
Ebb and Flow 113
Hainan 119
In Over My Head 127
Pieces to My Puzzle 135
That Unseen Hand 143
I'm Home 151
Epilogue 157
Endnotes 169
Acknowledgments 171
About the Author 173

Prologue

TO THIS DAY, MY LEAST FAVORITE QUESTION HAS ALWAYS BEEN one of the easy ones: "Where are you from?" I wonder why it matters where people are from. Why is it so important to identify someone, to label them as being from a certain place, to associate them with one dot on the map? There seems to be a basic need to identify a new acquaintance, to find out where their roots stem and why, even if it's just a small peek into why. Each time someone asks me that question, I typically proceed with the usual, "Well, I've lived all over." This answer rarely satisfies my inquirer. They want to know at least some of the places I've lived and what was the main cause for all the moves. When I add, "I grew up in Hong Kong," some immediately ask if my parents were military.

"No, my parents were Baptist missionaries but I was born in Tennessee."

The problem isn't the combination of odd locations or unexpected career fields, but then it is. Over the years, I've discovered that mentioning "missionary" in conjunction with "Hong Kong" does not provoke much dialogue. Rather, it often leaves a blank stare where there could be wonder and intrigue at the thought of a white American girl growing up in an exotic Asian metropolis. I wonder if it's due to a stigma over Baptists or missionaries or simply that my questioner is trying to remember which part of the world Hong Kong is in exactly. It could be that there's just too much information in those few details of my life. It's more than the usual explanation in reply to where one comes from. I've often thought it would be a lot easier to forget the past and just answer in an expected manner: "I'm from Tennessee," "West Texas," or "California." Each of these is technically true yet incomplete in and of itself.

Where you and I each began in life, what our parents were doing, where we grew up spending our formative, impressionable years—all of this leaves an imprint on who we are today. That, coupled with any sort of repetitive transitioning from one set of normal to a completely different set of normal, can make for a unique perspective, to say the least. That idea of belonging, whether strongly attached or detached from locations and family, means something deeper. The good news is, it can be unraveled and dissected in a healthy way when we look to the One who was there and continues to remain along our unique journeys. I love the idea of repurposing the script with Christ in his rightful place where he was all along.

In searching deeper through the recesses of my own memories, I like to ask myself what the Master and Commander of the universe was up to in my corner of the world—the world he formed and the spot I landed on. In sifting through those sometimes faint, sometimes remarkably clear recollections, I wonder how God was moving prior to and at the time of my arrival. Moving within boundaries, I inevitably became part of something bigger than myself—something I grew to accept as positive. There was always a greater narrative taking place, and looking back, I can see how he providentially sustained me within the context of my family. Through the varying circumstances in which I found myself, I had to learn to lift my gaze upward to seek him.

You have a story much like I do. As joyful or painful as it may be to unravel, it is one that can be redeemed, one that can lead you exactly to where you belong. If you do examine your past, as I have done in this book, I pray you'll see the many ways God had his hand on you as well.

My story begins long before my parents or I showed up on the scene, in a little-known region tucked between mossy, green mountains and a warm coastal sea breeze. Pieces of what look more like a story puzzle were scattered across a span of time, stretching further back than I can take credit for. I have come to see there is a connective thread of grace that offers an aerial glimpse into how the pieces are supposed to fit. I begin with turning the pages of history just enough to lay the edge pieces of my story's puzzle.

1
Kai Tak

THE TALE IS TOLD OF A CHINESE BELIEVER NAMED YAO JIAN Ming who moved with his family to Hong Kong in the 1930s. He settled down in what was then a poor, undeveloped area along Kowloon's sparsely populated mountain range. Ming happened to be a believer in *YeSou,* Jesus Christ. While getting acquainted with the locals, Ming discovered they had a village church with a lack of clear gospel teaching. It wasn't long before Ming invited a preacher to come teach the villagers of the redemptive work of Christ. The Bible was taught in Cantonese as well as in Swatow, a local dialect. In 1938, a building was constructed to house the growing church, including a place to baptize converts. A burden to reach out with both gospel and community services for the poor in the area developed. Once established, they called themselves the Swatow Baptist Church.

No one among the thriving congregation could have imagined their efforts would be astronomically disrupted and the newly built church torn down with the Japanese invasion of 1941. While World War II raged, many fled for safety. The village area at the base of Lion Rock Hill was cleared for the occupying army to fly in and land. By the providence of God, the spirit of the church was not crushed. Hong Kong may have fallen into the hands of the Japanese, but the Lord was preserving his people throughout that tempestuous period of time.[1]

In 1942 the Japanese army expanded Kai Tak Airport beneath the rugged mountain range. Many Allied POW (prisoner-of-war) laborers were used to construct two concrete runways. Numerous POW diary entries exist recalling the grueling work and long hours working on expanding Kai Tak.[2] During the process, the historic wall of the Kowloon Walled City and the 148-foot-tall Sung Wong Toi, a memorial for the last Song dynasty emperor, were destroyed for materials.[3]

It was in this very same region of Hong Kong, at this very same airport, that my story began, forty years later. God plucked up my family and me from small town middle America, and planted us right there in Kowloon. The region had not only come through recent wartime disaster, but it had transformed into a major international financial center, known worldwide as one of the wealthiest cities and tourist hot spots in Asia. My family's ministry would come to link hand in hand with what the Lord of the harvest was already doing among the Chinese people.

This is the story of a missionary daughter's firsthand experience of God's divine providence in a city that was changing from one identity to the next almost as often as she was. It's the filling in of a beautiful puzzle in which she had to figure out how she fit while settling on her own sense of belonging and identity.

"Where are we, Mommy?"

She didn't hear my timid voice, coming from below her trim waist. I yanked on her hand in mine and asked again.

"Mommy, where are we?"

She turned to look down at me, acknowledging my voice had been heard. Her face showed she was distracted with trying to keep up with Daddy and the boys. My little sister's legs straddled loosely around my mother's middle. Ruth's bare arms dangled at her sides as her sleepy head draped and bobbed over Mom's sagging shoulder. I felt a squeeze coming from my mother's clammy hand as she clasped a bit tighter and simultaneously pulled Ruth's limp body in and up with her other arm for a better hold. All the while, we were almost running forward as we followed the back of Daddy's predominant frame.

Strange sounds came from every direction. My ears caught a ringing chime coming from a speaker somewhere up high. A woman's voice followed the chime, but what was she saying? Her words sounded like a rapidly rising and falling pitch bearing no meaning. Was she singing or talking? Her announcement ended with that same ringing chime, and I liked the sound of it, but it stopped abruptly.

As we kept walking through the terminal, I turned to look at my mother to see if she could answer my question. Before I noticed, her legs had halted, and my four-year-old frame bumped up against her body and part of Ruth's shoe buckle. *Ouch!* Mom's skirt brushed smoothly over my face as if to say, "Be patient and wait!"

Where are we? I asked myself instead. Everything felt peculiar to me.

I lifted my free hand to rub my eyes, still not sure how real my surroundings were. My blond lashes opened wide, questioning eyes taking in the unusual view. I peered around the room, not remembering what had brought us here. All I could think of was my unanswered question.

May 6, 1982. My family and I had just landed at Kai Tak International Airport in Hong Kong. We were a family of six: Mom, Dad, my two older brothers, my younger sister, and me. Arriving at Kai Tak marked day one in my consciousness. This was the first day, the first chapter of a new beginning as a daughter of foreign-missionary parents. Someone was writing the story of my life, but who? Someone was nudging me to notice certain things and tuck them away in my memory bank. It wasn't my parents, nor my siblings. It wasn't anyone else physically present.

My family and I had traveled halfway around the globe, over an entire ocean—a very indirect, interconnected route from a modest American city of about 150,000 people to a metropolis off China's coast. We arrived at what was then a British Colony of five million. Its urban density averaged over forty-five thousand per square mile. Hong Kong is an English phonetic translation of its Cantonese name. The words *Hong* and *Kong* have no original English meaning—hence the funny sound to the Western ear when the two words are spoken together. At four and a half years old, I couldn't quite grasp what it all meant to be there and whether I felt good or bad about it.

Once we emerged on foot at our final destination, my understanding of what was happening in my life slowly lit up. It was as if I had tunneled through the experience blindly, and once I was deposited at Kai Tak, the light switch came on and with it, childlike wonder and awareness of my new surroundings. All memory of what we had just left behind meant nothing to me. All I could see and hear was the largeness of this strange, new place uniformly closing in on me. There was no looking back, no ability to connect what just happened from point A to point B.

As we made our way through the airport, a figure began

moving toward us with intention. I had a feeling he was coming straight toward my family and me on purpose. In my mind, my family and I were one unit, proceeding independently. Everyone on the scene before me became them versus us. No one felt familiar. People around us looked different from where we'd come from. Most of the people coming and going appeared to have a clearly defined resemblance—something that made me feel different from the crowd, like I'd entered a herd of a different breed, and I didn't quite belong. The reason for that resemblance was incomprehensible to me at four years old. Yet out of nowhere, a man had detached himself from "them" and was headed straight to "us" as though that had been his plan all day. How could this place produce someone who knew my family or could come alongside us when we'd come so far from the design of this presently constructed world?

I stuck close to my mother, clinging to the semblance of who I was within the context of my whole family. I had no reason not to trust and proceed. As though on cue, we weaved our way forward, willing to take the risk of intersecting with and receiving a stranger who had separated himself from all the others.

I swung my head around to see if I could make out the point from where we'd started walking. Was the entrance still open? Could we walk back through, get on the plane that dropped us off, and go back in reverse?

Coming in for landing just moments before, every person close enough to peer out one of the many windows on our jumbo jet likely would have been in awe, feeling a heightened sense of emotions ranging from thrill to sheer panic. Palms would have been gripping the ends of every armrest as our plane made a dramatic, low-altitude turning maneuver. Our plane, like all the others, had to make a sharp turn and begin its descent toward Kowloon Bay while flying over the surrounding mountains and then the city skyscrapers. It looked as though the rooftops of those buildings were at an arm's reach. We had flown over dozens of high-rise buildings, so close that it was possible for passengers on board to see people watching television inside their apartment homes. It would have felt too close for comfort for first timers like my family. High-rise apartments and tenements had sprung up to "within spitting distance" of the runway.[4]

Kowloon Bay was not a convenient location for landing large commercial aircraft, by any stretch of the imagination. *Kowloon* interestingly means "nine dragons," for eight mountains and an emperor. Avoiding all the natural and man-made structures was one thing, but also making sure the plane lined up with that tiny landing strip, where it jutted out onto Victoria Harbor on all three sides in any type of weather, was another level of skill. The strip was the one and only "Runway 13," and incoming pilots had to first look for the "checkerboard" to aid in navigating this approach. The well-known checkerboard was a vivid orange-and-white-checkered pattern painted on the side of a mountain.

Our pilots and perhaps many of the passengers may have known that this airport had been nicknamed "Kai Tak Heart Attack." Pilots of any size plane would have needed specific skills and piloting experience to attempt flying in or out of Hong Kong in those days. Kai Tak was in its heyday in the 1980s, having reached its boom years since original construction. When my family and I arrived, the international airport was taking on more flights than it was set up to handle.

For each passenger who took mental note, I would imagine coming in for landing was a hair-raising experience, followed by a huge sigh of relief once the plane touched down and came to a safe halt on solid ground. Unfortunately, or perhaps fortunately, this one remarkable event left no imprint on my mind at the time. In all of my parents' prior research, preparation, and correspondence regarding Hong Kong, did they know they were taking me and my three siblings to land on a piece of concrete ranked as the world's sixth most dangerous landing strip?

My parents' choices led us into a very humid and environmentally polluted—yet exotically industrialized—port colony off China's southeast mainland. The city showed up as merely a black dot on a world map. It was home to generations of Cantonese speakers who paid little notice to new Westerners who arrived, yet one lone man approaching seemed to have an idea who we were and why we'd come. All I knew was I was with my own small Texas tribe, and it felt as if we had uniformly landed on a completely different planet.

I like to think of it as life beginning for me at age four, three months and three weeks short of my fifth birthday to be exact. I had entered a world I only understood as being different. That difference would begin to change and reshape me whether I liked it or not.

2
Baucum Beginnings

A LONG-LOST MEMORY OPENED UP IN MY MOTHER'S MIND THE night I turned forty-five. She'd forgotten it until she saw a photo I texted to her on my birthday. Time and major life events had dismissed its strength long ago. In the picture, my husband and I were lying together, propped up and as cozy as can be in a single hospital bed as my husband received his initial treatment on the oncology floor at Penrose Hospital in Colorado Springs. I wore a sleeveless red summer dress speckled with white and gray flowers. I leaned my head on his left shoulder, content and restful. Brian's favorite trucker hat cast a shadow over his eyes. The port attached to his chest hung out at the neckline of his black workout shirt.

"I remember crawling into your hospital crib to curl up next to you," my mom reminisced over the phone. "It was draped in a covering, but I could climb in to feed you. It was tight for me to fit in there, but that was the only way to stay close enough to nurse. You were receiving treatment for . . . well, I don't remember what exactly, but you had to stay for, I think, a week."

"What? I can't believe I've never heard this before!" I exclaimed. "Was I sick? Are you sure you can't remember what I was in the hospital for? How come you and Dad have never told me this?" I was not angry. I was extremely interested, and with that interest came a barrage of questions, most for which neither of my parents had solid answers.

"I wish we could remember. You had some breathing trouble, probably the croup, so we had to stay and make sure you were all right," Mom confessed.

"The photo of you curled up close to Brian there in the hospital was so sweet, it took me back to when I had to climb into your crib in order to sustain your life. You were only one month old." My mom's voice was tender, and I could feel the heartbeat of a mother who loved her child deeply. She did what she could to remedy the physical separation in the days and nights during my hospital stay. I belonged to her, and she instinctively knew I would not thrive without her.

She and Daddy had labored with prayers and tears through my bout of sickness, so fragile a time as my life had just begun. A short-lived scare from long ago, and the only way I was going to hear about it was by walking through a current health scare with the person closest to me.

Like my mom, I knew exactly where I belonged in the moment.

I WAS MY PARENTS' THIRD CHILD, A WELCOMED FIRST LITTLE girl after two boys. I was also the biggest of them all, weighing in at a hefty ten pounds and two ounces. I arrived late, well past Mom's estimated due date. The doctor declared me healthy and strong. Nothing revealed that I'd soon be back in a hospital crib struggling to breathe. At twenty-three years old with two little boys and a newborn, my mother had her hands full. She still made time to record a few notes in a baby book for me.

Dad was a full-time graduate student. Outside of class, he worked odd jobs around the clock to support our family. Somehow he paid the bills and kept up his studies. My parents were not from Tennessee, but they received my birth certificate stamped and sealed from the Volunteer State.

Just two and a half years earlier, Mom and Daddy had heard a missionary couple speak at their home church in Amarillo, Texas, for the first time. The missionaries were about the same age as my parents, also raising young kids. As a family, they served in the jungles of Venezuela. Mom and Dad had never been exposed to foreign missions before and were extremely impressed that people would do that sort of thing for a living. Their worldview exploded. Being a missionary wasn't a business. It wasn't glamorous. It was a calling, something you do trusting, humbly serving God and God alone. That day marked a change in the trajectory of my parents' lives.

My dad sought counsel from their pastor. How could he be sure if what he and my mom felt was indeed a calling or just a good impression? The feeling was strong enough to pursue, but how? What should the first step be? The pastor advised my parents to study theology first, then seek where exactly God would lead them to serve. My parents enrolled at Tennessee Temple University, the same school their pastor had graduated from, simply because they did not know all the other options, nor did it make sense to waste time looking around. There was just one problem. They were not financially equipped to afford such a major transition. Then my dad remembered he had purchased land in New Mexico some years earlier. He decided to use the sale of the land to move out of state and get the family settled.

My parents were not alone in their big move to seminary. Others from their church also decided to go to TTU and excitedly made the transition. Many couples and individuals enrolled in the school during that era were inspired by a revival that had spread across the nation through the Billy Graham evangelistic ministry. They were energetic and hungry to learn more and passionate to serve not merely a religion or denomination but a real and personal Savior. Some, like my parents, were not financially set to make it long-term. It would require an even stronger passion and determination to finish what they'd started. Jobs were not abundant in a city like Chattanooga, even for college graduates. My dad held a bachelor's in political science, but the highest-paying jobs he could get offered little more than minimum wage. Students fell into community with one another, leaving groceries at each other's doorsteps when cupboards became bare and money short. There was nothing convenient about my coming into the world as the third baby to a family like mine. Hospital bills piled up. Sacrificing wherever possible was the only way to make those payments.

My parents chose my name, Faith, after my paternal grandmother suggested it. She saw the faith awakened in her son's heart and thought Faith would be an appropriate name for his daughter. My parents liked the suggestion, then went on to choose my middle name, Jeanine. They chose that name in honor of a missionary—a woman they admired who displayed great faith in going with her husband to live and minister in a jungle among tribal Indians.

Dad and Mom were not pastors' kids or some great Christian leaders' kids who had their path paved or directed for them. Their parents did not coax them to put God first in their career choices. Nobody urged my parents to go evangelize the great wide world. These two individuals acted upon a strong internal tug to serve Jesus Christ in whatever capacity he directed them. They had each been raised hearing about God, all the while their hearts void of any personal relationship with him. They believed in him as the Creator yet hadn't volitionally accepted Jesus as Lord and Savior of their own lives. Hurting from unresolved conflicts in their family relationships, they indulged in partying, sex, drugs, all the vices most of their peers turned to for fulfillment and belonging. Through a series of events, my newlywed parents were introduced to Christ, and together they laid down their burden of sin at the cross, confessing their need for and trust in Jesus alone.

When I showed up, a forward momentum was present that has not stopped even to this day.

After graduating with a master of divinity, my dad moved our family back home to Texas. My dad signed up with an independent Baptist mission board. The board would guide him and my mom through all the logistics of becoming full-time missionaries. They learned that life was not going to slow down after graduation. The mission board asked them to attend conferences and an intensive linguistics school, set up a new finance and retirement plan, and create family prayer cards along with a ministry presentation. They also gave my parents a financial goal they would have to meet, or come close to meeting, in order to begin work overseas. Dad began calling area churches for an invitation to present his ministry plan. He circled in dates on the calendar with speaking engagements. Slowly but surely, a growing handful of churches and individuals began giving to the Baucum ministry.

A theme of giving and belonging to a higher calling was part of my upbringing. It began with my parents giving of themselves, their ideas of what a good life sounded like, and laying that all on the line for the sake of the gospel. My parents identified with a cause they believed was greater than themselves.

I was born to a couple that was wholeheartedly preparing for full-time ministry. By the time I was three, they knew where we were going and approximately when we would arrive. I would be given the opportunity to grow up in a third culture, twice removed from my parents' individual cultures.

Missionaries' children are impacted more than any others over the course of the mission. A book I read about a fellow missionary kid's experience described a common path third culture kids traverse all because of the choices their parents make. It is beautiful and raw, summing up my own background:

> Our journey often begins through the faith and calling of our parents, rooted in the past but grown and sustained through our own decisions of faith.
>
> We were molded and shaped by parents who loved us and were called to a work that included a bigger, broader world, a world where "nine to five" or "weekend" were unknown. And in some families, the broader, bigger world won. And the children lost. They were sacrificed to a greater commission, a higher calling of well-meaning parents whose hearts flamed with passion.
>
> They too lived between the broader world of being a part of a mission community and the smaller world of us, the Brown Family. I know what a struggle it is to live out a faith that is winsome, not destructive, to live out a passion for God that brings the family alongside, not sprawled in the dust.[5]

My mother's hand yanked at mine, pulling my attention forward.

"Keep up, Faith! We have to keep moving!"

My pulse quickened as my eyes darted back toward the direction we were moving as a family. There would be no more checking out what was behind. We'd made too many turns and maneuvered through mazes of people anyhow.

My family quietly entered the bustling city undoubtedly with many others for the first time that day. We had not made any headlines. We were no celebrity family. Just two ordinary adults with their four young kids disembarking a Korean airline flight that had connected from Seoul. Two adult, four child tickets. Luggage piling out of cargo and onto the conveyor belt at baggage claim. I don't know what the weight limit and rules were back in those days, but judging from future travels my family made, I know our stash of luggage was always a sight to behold.

Four American youngsters accompanied by their parents got their passports stamped for first-time entry approval that day in May. Ross was the oldest at eight, less than two weeks away from his ninth birthday. With his thick, dark brown hair and brown eyes, there was no mistaking him as his mother's son. Ross was a stockier build than the rest of us. Six-year-old Timmy and I could have been mistaken for twins. Two skinny green-eyed redheads, nineteen months apart. Ruthie was two. She had brown eyes and wispy, light brown hair, much easier to manage than the mop on my head.

Ross might have been deemed old enough to carry his own passport as we shuffled through customs. Dad kept the rest out of reach from us younger kids. Those first couple of stamps would multiply in the years to come. Becoming an international traveler at such a young age would contribute to a major identity shift away from how I would have grown up viewing myself had we stayed in southwestern USA. Instead, stepping away from one culture and into another brought my identity in line with the inescapable worldview that had just opened up for me.

I would soon learn that each of us would be labeled the *gweilo* or *laowai,* the slang terms that translated to mean "ghost person," "foreign devil," or "old foreigner," depending on whether the Chinese spoken was Cantonese or Mandarin. That was the name-calling we received until we became friends. After that it became commonplace vocabulary. Apart from tourists and business travelers, Western residents were few in number in comparison to the population, particularly outside of Kowloon. We were on *their* turf, and though we were accepted and free to come and go, there would be that outward awareness that we originally belonged to another country. Over time, I would learn to adapt to this new environment, call it home, and begin thinking like the people I came to live among.

The spring of '82 turned out to be a monumental, eye-opening experience for me. Maybe that's why I remember it so clearly. But why can't I bring up memories of the exciting plane ride or cramming in that tiny van that took us to our new neighborhood? There would have been so much to see out the windows as we made our way through crowded, winding streets, pedestrians everywhere. How come I only recall a few moments throughout all the traveling? What makes the mind grasp certain things and ignore the rest? That first, long trip stands out in my dad's mind. But he and Mom were adults; I, a very young child, simply following their lead, easily, willingly, safely.

Perhaps if I had carried something sentimental from home,

feelings and thoughts generated from what that item meant would have been my connective link from the previous to the new.

Tucked comfortably on one side of his body, under one bony arm, Timmy carried a special cushion. I knew it was special because he cherished it. The off-white square pillow had a picture of a red schoolhouse surrounded by black stitching. Timmy's kindergarten teacher back home had all her students' little names sewn on the soft fabric for Timmy to remember his friends from his first year in school. Each name was sentimental to my brother. Every hand-formed letter would remind him of someone real, someone he knew from the place that had all but vanished from my mind. Even the warm, dry grassy scent it carried within its cotton stuffing reminded him of what he'd left behind. That wide-open-plains scent was nowhere to be found in our new, sticky, sea-dwelling place of arrival.

I wasn't jealous of his pillow, nor do I remember ever holding it close, but I did come to learn of its purpose, which was to bring up sweet memories in Timmy's mind, to show him tangibly how much he meant not only to his classmates but to his teacher. Timmy had a group, a tribe if you will, that loved him and would miss him. That alone was special and unique.

Our first trip to Hong Kong marked so much more than a day on the calendar in 1982. It marked deeply on the hearts and lives of an unlikely, unassuming American family, so unaware of what the future held. Every turn of a corner, every next minute had something each of us needed to watch out for, to learn, to claim. What would be my next surprise? What would I reach out and grab to ground me there? What would become familiar first among the myriad of unfamiliarity and language barriers?

3
The Upstairs Window

It wasn't that high. Only the first floor aboveground in a twenty-story building. The living room window immediately drew me to its side. The vantage point was convincing to a four-year-old. I needed an open view, any view. Having just arrived at our new apartment—what the Europeans called a flat—I stood peering out the framed window. The atmosphere all around me was calm. I felt okay, quieted, and at rest. We had left the busy public places. The cosmos had stopped moving for a moment. I took in the new scenery that would adorn my world for the next three years.

Our flat at 32B First Floor Nassau Street, Mei Foo Sun Chuen, Kowloon, Hong Kong, might as well have been my first home ever, because I have never been able to remember the houses I lived in before that one. It was like everything else that simply didn't matter anymore.

My family and I moved into Hong Kong's first large-scale private housing estate. In the early '80s, Mei Foo Sun Chuen was considered to be an affluent, middle-class residential development. The last stages of building had been completed only four years prior to our arrival. There were older sections where construction had begun in 1968. Mei Foo covered forty acres with a total of ninety-nine towers. The Chinese translation of the four words: Mei Foo Sun Chuen literally means "beautiful, trust or belief in, new estate." It makes sense that one of the streets was named after the island of Nassau in the Bahamas, a beautiful, desirable location. Many Mei Foo residents enjoyed scenic ocean views. My family did not attain an ocean view flat. Our building was tucked somewhere close to the estate's center.

Tall beige buildings accented with green and crowned with brown trim stood packed in tight, casting long shadows over the ground we walked. Suffering from a sunburn was not an issue while living at Mei Foo estates. If we wanted to be out enjoying clear skies and cheery sunshine, we had to be out at high noon or, as my mother recalls, we were left searching for narrow slivers of sunlight streaming through buildings. Our neighborhood did not offer wide open places to walk and play. There were no grassy lawns to tend to or stretches of fields separating buildings. We would not hear a lawn mower for the duration of our stay or smell the scent of freshly mowed grass wafting through the breeze.

My favorite part of Mei Foo was the common area, a walkway to the little shops. The entire area was all gray cement, but its landmark exhibit displayed a clear, shallow man-made stream that flowed and pooled over a cement floor. Various fountains spouted intermittently like miniature aquatic fireworks into the air. A bright red oriental-style bridge arched cheerfully over the brook, beckoning me to skip up and over to the other side. The red bridge proudly distinguished the center of Mei Foo.

My new neighborhood housed some seventy to eighty thousand residents. Overall, it was a major jolt moving from a place where personal space is enjoyed and a necessary way of life to a compact, upward-built city where elbow room is not expected. Mentally processing the difference took some time. Living and breathing in such close proximity to so many other people was a completely new experience. "Community" took on a whole new meaning.

My parents learned about Mei Foo from corresponding with a Chinese man who was associated with our mission board. To me, he was a mystery man. As I mentioned in chapter 1, he welcomed us at the airport's Arrivals Hall, politely greeting my parents in English. I remember him walking forward and presenting himself to my family, detached from all the other strangers. I had no idea how someone could possibly know us there, but my mind interpreted his presence as friendly and safe.

Our flat was previously occupied by an anonymous missionary family. We were the new rotation, ultimately following a long line of Protestant missionaries from the West. On the inside, the apartment appeared modest and small by American standards. The size of our apartment never bothered me, nor did the appearance of the bedrooms. What stands out in my memory was the window that looked out at other buildings all around us and, most of all, down several feet to the pavement. I could see a few ornamental plants, a parking lot, and people, all of them with jet-black hair. The elevated compact house situated among all the other elevated homes felt unfamiliar and unsteady. My instincts pulled me close to the window. At least there I could get a sense of where I was in relation to my world that had dramatically transformed.

We had brought no furniture, only clothing and essentials in our suitcases. My parents had not shipped crates of home goods to furnish our new home, as they had been promised a furnished apartment. The previous tenants had moved out weeks before our arrival, leaving the place unattended to collect dust and mold. The latter quickly spread its ugly spores around the abandoned kitchen. Poor Mom! Much to her dismay, upon looking around her new cooking space, she discovered thick black mold on the walls and inside the refrigerator. Mold would be a quiet new pest that my mother would seek to quell as often as it showed up. Coming from a very dry climate in northwest Texas, she was not used to such a nasty intruder. Hong Kong had the perfect humidity levels to encourage mold's sporous growth.

The Barnards from Michigan—fellow missionaries—showed up at our door to introduce themselves and welcome us to the neighborhood. Our first visitors were not Chinese. It didn't matter how they knew we'd just moved in. What did matter were the smiles on their pale faces and the fact that they spoke English. Their friendly demeanor meant something to me. Some of the children stood at eye level with me. There were several girls and only one boy. Since they lived in a "next-door" building, we kids would spend countless fun-filled hours at play. We would also attend school together. God must have known we needed other Americans close by. He blessed us with Christian fellowship on our first day in Mei Foo. Settling in wouldn't seem so hard after all. I truly appreciated the gift of their friendship more and more as time went on.

The presence of this other missionary family at our door pierced through the foreign veil that had fallen over me, allowing me to acknowledge and make sense of the unfamiliar. My new world and my spot in it didn't seem so bad after all. I have no idea what our parents conversed about as they stood there at our door. I was still standing over by the window.

Soon after our eventful first day, I became aware of a smaller window, the one in my bedroom. I sat up in the top bunk gazing at movements below, at eye level, as well as those reaching high above, further than I could crank my neck to see. Most of the time I felt like a bird in her comfy nest, peering down at passersby as well as trying to make out what other families were doing in all those flats across the way. Window after window stacked up endlessly as far as I could see. Every level in every direction represented others who lived their lives within those confines. People walked by below, occupied with their own thoughts and conversations. I enjoyed the show while sitting comfortably. It was there in that top bunk that I first imagined my future. What would it be like to be a woman? What would it be like to be a grown-up? Would I like the difference, or would it be weird? Of course, that future time seemed too far off to feel as real as my present.

What sparked the curiosity? I now wonder. Perhaps it was my ever-expanding world on display right there from my new bedroom. Instead of entertainment on a screen, I developed an interest in the view beyond my living space. Windows offered an inescapable peek into who I was in the sense of a broader universe and why I mattered there.

I SLEPT ON THAT TOP BUNK EVERY NIGHT. THERE WAS NO SUCH thing as central cooling or heating in residential homes. Instead, bulky boxed air conditioner units sat in a corner of bedroom windows. By early May, Hong Kong's subtropical climate boasted high humidity caked with suffocating heat. Thankfully, it was also the beginning of monsoon season. The rain cooled the air but also left a sticky sweat between my skin and clothing. Skin stayed perpetually hydrated in those conditions while air conditioning units worked like magic to dry out the air.

Night after night my parents showed up in the same dream. They would be standing there, not doing much, available to meet my needs. Just before I would open my mouth to speak to them, before I would start walking toward them, another man and woman would show up. They mingled about casually. As they mingled, I would lose track of which of the four people were my parents. Every time, I was taken aback. Fear peaked at the sight of another man and woman who mirrored my mom and dad. The two couples created two identical sets of parents. Fear loomed larger, an unwelcome presence in my dream, clenching, constraining.

I was afraid I would choose the wrong set and I'd be sorry. Sorry for not being able to choose my real parents and sorry for picking the fake ones, certain enemies in disguise even though they appeared the same outwardly. I didn't know how bad the intruders were, but I felt certain they would not love me like my real parents. If I chose them, I wouldn't belong. I couldn't make the mistake of choosing wrong, but it felt impossible. There was no one to guide me by the hand or offer any clues. I had to squirm my way out of the confusing dream.

At last, I would wake up, thankful to hear the air conditioner humming at the window. Not a hint of daybreak, but I would strain my ears to hear my sister breathing steadily just below me. I would arch my back over the top bunk rail, peering down through the dark, making out a small form under a patched quilt.

I would slump my head back onto my pillow and let out an exhale. All was well. My family was still the same. I hadn't lost my parents, even though I couldn't see them in their room, our door closed. I knew they were there. My sister's presence confirmed it.

The pressure of the night would ease off, allowing daybreak. The sun slowly but surely lifted the weight of the dark, as well as the isolating fear that had tried to take over. My sister would stir, and the day always began after my troubling dream. I didn't tell anyone. It always evaporated from my mind altogether once the day began.

The next time the twin parents appeared in my dreams, the same insecure feelings arose. Why do they all look the same, and how could I know which are my real parents? Something about being displaced, life disrupted, needing more security in where and to whom I belonged put the dream on repeat for a couple of years.

4
Church

I HUNCHED AGAINST A FLAT PEW IN THE CHURCH BALCONY overlooking the backs of the congregation, my brothers on either side of me, fingers grasping a slip of paper and a crayon. My attention was pulled away from my coloring to what was happening below. The minister's discourse fell silent, and a reverent hush took over from down below all the way up to where I sat with my family.

"Faith!" my mother whispered. Her index finger curled in motion for me to come toward her. I shuffled around Ross's bumpy knees, and Mom pulled me up onto her lap.

The Lord's Supper had begun. The ushers slowly made their way down each aisle, pausing at each pew to administer the elements. As I sat still, quietly and somberly watching the communion procedures, my mother's voice began again, this time close to my ear. My brain zeroed in to collect her words, recognizing they were designed for my understanding and knowledge. I did not turn to look into her face as she whispered. My eyes continued to follow the movements below until heavy footsteps sounded behind us, jerking my head away from Mom's voice momentarily to catch a glimpse of who was walking by. A man strode forward, holding a shiny platter. He bent slightly to offer its contents to people awaiting their turn.

My mom spoke low as if she were telling me a secret. She described what was on that platter and the one that came next, then explained why she and others partook of each. The reverent meaning and purpose of this moment was brought to life as she spoke. The mystery of the cross unfolded in a way that I could grasp. My spiritual eyes were coaxed open to see Jesus as Savior, a Lamb slain for the sins of the world. This special "supper" was meant to remind God's people, no matter where they lived, of the sacrifice once made on their behalf, in remembrance, in gratitude. She saw with Holy Spirit wisdom and prudence that I was old enough to receive what she wanted to convey.

That precious experience was one of the biggest influences in my life that led me to desire God as a child and ever since.

We initially began attending what looked to me like a very large church. Other Westerners attended besides my family. My parents decided we would attend the English services on Sunday mornings for the sake of maintaining regular corporate worship. This experience put us into an expatriate world within the larger Chinese world we had entered and were still trying to figure out.

I never comprehended a word the pastor spoke from the pulpit during Sunday services. There was no escaping to children's classes or junior church. The platform, pulpit, and preacher seemed distant and out of touch with who we were and why we were there as we sat and watched from up high in the balcony section. We did not sit on the ground level, closer to the pulpit, and I wonder if having four wiggly children had something to do with that.

Hong Kong in the '80s was already very familiar with

Christianity, Catholicism, and a variety of other "foreign" religions. The locals knew what missionaries were and why they came. The Bible had already been translated into Cantonese and was easily accessible at local Christian bookstores and nonprofit ministries.

My dad was connected to a smaller Chinese church through our mission board. It was a local ministry, but we did not yet speak Cantonese. Time and serious study were necessary for the adults who hoped to share the gospel message freely. We children were exposed to our second language at the best time of our lives due to the environment in which we lived. Besides Ruth, who received formal lessons at her Chinese preschool, my brothers and I did not receive any intentional study of Cantonese the first three years. What we did possess was a natural ability to hear and distinguish the sounds and tones spoken all around us. A child's capacity to make sense of what is heard from the shop clerk haggling with customers, to casual good morning greetings or inquiring if someone had eaten yet, left us blissfully unaware of the enormous amount of language learning that was actually taking place. We were immersed and took in everything through our senses, making valuable connections between what was heard, seen, smelled, tasted, and touched each and every day.

The big English church was a traditional, established denominational church. The services went long, and I'm sure I must have slept through quite a few. Thankfully, it had a little playground outside on the property. An awning blocked the hot sun as we children ran to play outside in the humidity that first summer each Sunday after the service.

Going to church was good for me in that it offered more "Christian" familiarity connecting us with where we had come from. I was never asked whether I wanted to go. Because of my parents' priorities, I was never disconnected from any church. It was another place where I came to feel that I belonged, whatever it looked and sounded like, however often the location changed.

I SOON LEARNED THAT NOT ALL CHURCH FRIENDSHIPS WERE healthy and profitable. One night we had a new family over for dinner, and I remember connecting the dots with how we knew them. The children played with us on that church playground. Two of the boys were the same ages as me and my sister.

The four of us played House in our bedroom with the door closed, lights off. My brothers must have been occupied elsewhere, as they were nowhere to be found as far as I was concerned. In the continuation of our little game, my sister ended up on the top bunk, while I stayed on the bottom, each of us with a son of the new church family.

All of a sudden, in whatever role I was playing—mother, daughter, wife, I have no idea, but the latter would be my best guess—the boy on my bunk asked me to take off my shirt. In my not-yet-five-year-old consciousness, I felt an immediate halt, the impression that it wasn't right for him to ask me that. I knew my shirt was there for a purpose, and I didn't go around taking it off for anybody. In that moment, I froze between the red flag in my conscience and the boy's request. The bedroom was dark; no one could see. That cover of darkness felt safe enough in my own room with friends my parents allowed. The mood shifted from pure, innocent fun to suddenly awkward.

Before I could make a decision or answer with my words or actions, the door swung wide open and light streamed in.

Mom stood tall and authoritative in the doorway, as indeed she was to us mischievous children. With one quick flick of a finger, light slammed out the dark, eight little eyelids squinting in response. Somehow she knew exactly when to shed light on the situation, forever sparing me the dismal discomfort I came face-to-face with in that childish game. "Even a child is known by his doings, whether his work be pure, and whether it be right," the Proverb says (Proverbs 20:11).

The accountability for all four of us children became present through the appearance of a parent standing at the door. The innocent game escalating toward something unhealthy was easily and quickly averted that night. I'm thankful for the episode and what I learned from it. The Lord was good to me through his provision of authority, no matter how harmless it might appear to others. My ability to consider; instinct powered by conscience; was sharpened in a small but beneficial way at such a young age. That would serve me well for a lifetime.

AFTER ATTENDING THE ENGLISH SERVICES FOR A FEW MONTHS, we moved to a fully Cantonese church. My parents were connected with the pastor through our mission board. Reverend Ernest Loong had established Witness Baptist Church in 1961. My parents were prepared and ready for this move. It was not a difficult transition, but it was our third church within a few months' time. It would be the type of missionary work they could glean from. It would prepare them for starting a church plant in the next few years.

Reverend Loong was a stoic, elderly gentleman, always wearing a gray suit. He spoke fluent English and allowed my parents to assist in the ministry. He wasn't grandfatherly in my view, but rather maintained a courteous demeanor. His wife was plump and kind.

Reverend Loong prayed a grave benediction over his flock at the close of each service. It was the same every time, but the best part was the manner in which he spoke, lifting his arms in blessing. My brothers and I picked up the long, drawn-out Chinese terms at the tail end, mimicking the phrases at home. If my parents ever reproved us for mocking, it never sunk in or made a difference. That one ecclesiastical prayer, though undervalued by the American children in attendance, also came to define the minister. Almost like an Old Testament prophet coming to life, it characterized as well as memorialized the first real Chinese pastor in my life.

At some point my dad was able to speak from his pulpit and even preach entire messages in Cantonese. I do not remember feeling impressed by my dad's incredible accomplishment, but I know it was huge. He went from being born and bred in the panhandle of Texas to living in Hong Kong, speaking one of the most ancient and complex tonal languages in the world. I don't believe it was because he particularly loved the challenge or wanted the most difficult tasks; I think he was just trying to achieve the goal, which was to preach the gospel to the people in their own language. He had also grown up with a strong work ethic, and that kept him from quitting.

Before Dad had the opportunity to speak or preach in Cantonese, he sat and listened to the Cantonese preaching from Pastor Loong. He watched and learned the way the services were led. He was not there to take over this ministry or "Americanize" it. He was there to partner with this church of like faith until he and Mom could branch out and establish a new local church. Church planting was his aim and calling. It was what he would write about for years to come in his newsletters that he sent back home to supporting churches. I can see my young father sitting there on the front row, the only white man in the congregation, trying to pick out learned words and phrases. Everything would have sounded like they were speaking way too fast until finally, as it got to sound more and more familiar, the speed "slowed" to what felt like a normal, natural pace. I know because I've sat in various congregations trying to pick out those words. It's exhausting brain work, but helpful for learning new languages.

My mom studied the language just as hard, but she was not called to preach, nor did she believe that was a woman's role in the church. Instead, she took on the task of teaching a children's class.

I have some old photos of that first class. Small kids sat nicely in attendance, neat and tidy on toddler-sized red plastic chairs. Mom taught Bible stories, doing her best to use Cantonese words and phrases she had learned from her own study time. Some of the other mothers participated in guiding the younger children. I was a big kid compared to the toddlers and younger children in the room. My older brother Tim was a helper. Our involvement gave me the sense that we were on the same team as helpers. We sang songs with hand motions to visualize the meaning of the lyrics. Mom made the class fun. I'm sure she had only a few of the usual abundant American materials and curriculum designed to aid children's Sunday school teachers. As an attendee, I didn't notice any lack. All we children needed were the joy and nurturing guidance she gave each week. Little did I know that was the first of many Sunday school classes and ministry opportunities my siblings and I would participate in—my parents leading, us kids involved and making every effort, with their guidance, to have a part in ministering to people. It became a way of life.

The photos I have in my plain white photo box labeled "Hong Kong" help solidify the recollections I muse over. Children colored pages like any children's class would, followed by a simple craft. An open window in the background of one of the photos reveals there was no view (as usual), only pipes and buildings just a few feet away. Thin, metal bars covered every window, signifying another cultural difference we were not used to, coming from middle-class America. Some of the bars were pushed out in order to hang clothes. Others were unmovable or locked in place.

Bars on windows didn't hinder our lessons in that room. They were simply a reminder of where we were. Hong Kong had a high crime rate (but low violent crime), linked to the widespread criminal organizations known as triads. I would later become very familiar with the name of the local *Hak-sehwui,* or "Black Society." As I grew up, my brothers and their friends would often joke about them in Chinese lingo, teasing each other of being in a triad as if the groups were harmless or fake. I would come to learn that triads were a serious concern and that teen boys often got recruited into these societies if they and their families were not careful. Triads had a long history beginning in mainland China, and Hong Kong gang members had come to organize their own territorial groups around the city. The British government was intolerant of these secret societies and considered the triads a criminal threat.

Of course, none of that ever crossed my mind as to why the bars were a window feature in our church apartment. We mingled and had class weekly in small, cage-like spaces. I was completely unaware of crime or the threat of crime until much later. I'm glad my innocence was protected, and I never felt unsafe within the confines of those rooms. The city was largely a safe place to be out, day or night.

What I loved most about Witness Baptist Church were the young adults who quickly latched on to my family. Mak, Serena, Patti, and others whose names I can't recall visited with us at church, showering us kids with attention and practicing their English. They visited us in our home too. These personal connections did more than offer temporary friendships; they created a needed attachment and sense of belonging that were so important to our ability to thrive on the mission field. I regretted having to go to bed while Mom and Dad stayed up visiting with a group around our dining room table. That was the worst for any kid! The house would be dark, lights off except for the dining room and kitchen. I would peer longingly toward the dining room table, lit with a glow of warm friendships, smiling back at me with their goodnight wishes.

I don't know all of the stories of how each of those people came to be members at Witness, but they were there, and my family and I enjoyed each one of them. Mak became like an uncle to us kids. He was single and wore wide-framed glasses. He had some height to his slender frame. Clothed in the typical white, short sleeved, open collar shirt over a flat, bare chest, he always kept the shirt tucked into belted, breezy dark slacks. Mak looked the part of a classic Hong Kong fellow of that era. He clearly enjoyed being friends with my dad and our family. He had a passion for photography and carried his camera on a wide shoulder strap everywhere we went together. I don't think my parents owned a camera, so I'm so grateful for the photos he took. We still have the prints he developed for us. One of my favorites is an eight-by-ten close-up of me. I'm looking up into the camera, standing in front of a kiddie ride at Chuck E. Cheese. The lighting is aglow with my sweet smile, the joy in my eyes. I wore a dark coat, and my pose reflects the trust I had in my photographer.

God brought special individuals into our lives throughout our years of ministry. It was always someone who stuck around for a while, invested in us, and vice versa. God blessed us by providing so many people who felt like family. People we would have never known were it not for my parents making that giant move to another spot on the globe. Mom and Dad's mind-set was always centered on building relationships, leading people to a saving faith in Christ and discipling them. My mind-set was just about being a kid. I liked having fun people around. They were the ones whom my whole family bonded with and who made saying good-bye brutal when it came time to take a furlough back to the States. They were the ones who made Hong Kong feel like home. It was their home, and they not only allowed us to be there; they accepted us. We were the minority—the new Western family trying to fit in, to belong, to learn the culture, and to love the people.

5
Beacon Hill

I STARED DOWN AT MY HANDWRITING PAGE. IT WAS ALMOST completely blank, but the lines stared impatiently up at me. They demanded words, much like my teacher had demanded as she marched through the classroom, passing out papers. Her instructions were clear and to the point: write a creative story using correct punctuation, then get in line to turn it in at her desk. The weight of this assignment made my pencil feel heavy in my hand. I looked around at my uniformed classmates. They were all hunched over their pages, writing feverishly. No one wanted to be last in line lest they get a scolding from Mrs. Stout.

Next to me sat my best friend, Amy. Her long brown curls grazed her page as she wrote word after word in her pretty handwriting. Everything about Amy was pretty. Her eyes radiated joy and confidence. She wasn't afraid of anything. She loved school and everyone at school. Her curly bangs framed her face like a doll. She may as well have been a real-life doll from a toy store. I was glad we were best friends. My favorite part of school? She and I got to be desk mates.

Amy's natural energy motivated me to get busy writing. I penciled in something about going to the park with my family. It sounded good. I scratched out another sentence or two. I glanced up at Mrs. Stout's desk. She was sitting there, facedown, shuffling papers. As soon as she looked up, I immediately diverted my eyes down to my page. *How do I finish it? Is this enough? Will she be pleased with my work?* I wondered. It needed a closing, but I was stuck. I had writer's block at seven years old. In a flash, a thought crossed my mind: my desk mate might be able to help, but we weren't allowed to talk. Without saying a word, I noticed Amy lift her pencil, exhaling a contented sigh at her brilliant handiwork. There, in block letters, at the very bottom of her page was the phrase "The End."

That's it! I immediately copied the phrase, added a full stop, then silently set down my pencil and quickstepped to get right behind my best friend in a line that was forming quickly. I patiently awaited my turn, gleeful at my accomplishment, proud of my story with the perfect ending. I was not last in line. Others got behind me. All was well in the world. I breathed deeply.

FOR THREE YEARS, MY BROTHERS AND I ATTENDED BEACON Hill, a large international elementary school established in 1967. It had opened with the purpose of educating non-Cantonese-speaking students as well as local children who could speak a good level of English. The student body consisted of children from all over the world. A few of us were American, plenty were British and European, while others were Indian or Pakistani. All the teachers whom I remember were from the United Kingdom.

I was so excited the first day of school after adjusting to Hong Kong that first summer of '82. In a photo snapped of me and my siblings, I stood exuding happiness. It was early in the morning, but sunshine lit my smile, and I stood tall in my sleeveless, pink-and-white-checkered uniform dress. It was light and airy, pleated at the waist. My full hair was brushed clean of tangles around my shoulders, pulled up in side barrettes. I felt ready to bounce off like a bunny to my next adventure. My brothers wore their pressed white dress shirts and gray shorts with long socks, very British looking.

Prior to this, I had never attended kindergarten, preschool, or even day care. My first introduction to the world of academia was Beacon Hill off Beacon Hill Road in Kowloon. I had been excited to go to "big school" with my brothers. We were a team, all dressed in uniform, ready to go and learn together. Once we arrived at school, though, we dispersed, each ushered away to his or her appropriate class. I lost touch with my teammates. I was used to my siblings and me dispersing at times, but that permanent consignment of classes by age was another dimension. The body of students was too large for me to keep track of where each of us Baucum kids fit.

I never got used to the yelling and shouting that came from my superiors at the front of the classroom facing the students. The old lady with the white bun yelled the worst. Her face turned so red, even blue, in her vehement commands, I thought her head might pop off. I never quite understood what made the ladies so angry. Now that I'm a teacher myself, I suppose it had to have been all the perceived classroom disruptions and discipline problems. Yelling and screaming was how those teachers handled their classes. I was not used to ever hearing adults shouting ferociously at me or any other kids. Some children tune out that type of communication, but I never could. It bothered me, so I submitted and stayed quiet for them. I'm not sure why I never mentioned it to my parents or sought their comfort. My mother would ask me how school went, and I consciously kept my bad feelings of the day to myself.

Recess was always a favorite. Students spread like ants, covering every corner of the concrete grounds. Our play area was walled in by the towering seven-story school building. If it rained, we played under the part of the building that held its first floor aboveground. Playing in paved spaces underneath and surrounded by overbearing skyscrapers became the norm.

I do not recall seeing either of my brothers at recess or anywhere else on the school grounds. We rode the bus together and went home together, but they may as well have been on another planet in their classrooms on different floors. It wasn't that I missed them, but it does seem unfortunate how we were so separated, the school being so large. I wasn't known to have brothers or recognized as being the sister of Ross and Timmy. The opportunity to point out to classmates who my siblings were across the room never presented itself.

During school-wide gatherings, which were a common occurrence, I stayed seated with my own class. Sometimes I took part in school plays there in the large auditorium. Kids who had birthdays during the school year were acknowledged with a giant, fake, multicolored, though slightly hideous, birthday cake rolled in on a cart. Timmy and Ross each had birthdays during the school year, but mine was during summer break.

I learned the song "Raindrops Keep Fallin' on My Head" for a school play and was given a kid-size umbrella for a prop. I stood squished in tight among many of my peers, holding a rainbow-hued covering that matched the other kid's umbrellas. I liked how mine made me feel enclosed and protected under its arched shadow. The popular song we sang was catchy, and I enjoyed hearing the tune, singing along with the other performers. A warm, fuzzy feeling from the easy cadence of our theme song flooded my mind. I imagined raindrops falling from the ceiling onto the stretched lining over my head. What more that particular play included, I have no idea. Its melody whisked me off into dreamland, and nothing else mattered. During the show and practice times, I stood on that stage free of stage fright. There were too many of us to fuss over who was getting the attention. Being packed in felt more comfortable than standing alone.

Unbeknownst to me, God was there, considering, pondering his work in my young life. In his goodness, he blessed me with a special playmate whose light shined brighter than any other I knew. Amy and her family had arrived in Hong Kong shortly after we did. I don't recall when our families first met, but I do know that she quickly became my new best friend. Ages and birthdays are a highlight to kids, so I learned she was a bit older than me, but we were still in the same grade. I needed to be there in the same class with Amy. God had prepared my heart to recognize something that she had but I did not. My sweet friend confidently announced one day at recess in her beautiful and girlish way that she was a Christian. She was proud of it and wanted the world to know. I may or may not have been the only one who went home that day and asked her parents what that meant and if she could be one too.

I recognized the light of Jesus in my friend and went straight to someone who would explain how I could have it as well. My dad was pleased to point me to the Source. He dropped what he was doing to open God's Word and read me the scriptures I needed to hear that day. With wisdom, he saw that his daughter was seeking something she knew about but had not yet claimed for herself. My dad showed me the way to become a "Christ follower." Yes, a little girl who recognized the difference between good and bad needed to see the Savior who made a way to the Father. The time my dad took to show me how to pray and ask to be saved created a memory I've never forgotten. That childlike faith must have been so pleasing to him as well as the One who stood waiting to draw me in.

As I stepped forward, placing my story page into Mrs. Stout's outreached hand, I smiled with the confidence of a young writer proud of her work. I felt pleased with my story, especially the ending statement which was the perfect touch, just like Amy's. Plus, I'd drawn a picture of my family at the top. It was personal and it was all mine. I just needed to turn and walk away once I got an approving nod.

Mrs. Stout did not look up at me. Instead, her eyebrows went askew.

"You copied Amy."

It was a statement, not a question; an accusation, not an inquiry.

Mrs. Stout publicly instructed me to collect all my desk supplies and move immediately to the empty seat beside Simon.

At the expectation of praise, I received a rebuke with the worse consequence ever—having to sit by a boy. My teacher might as well have told me to go sit by an alien. Copying the words "The End" turned out to be the tipping point. She decisively cut me loose from the one person I had tethered myself to. I did not know what to think of this new arrangement, whether I deserved it or whether Mrs. Stout was simply the cruelest person on the planet. No longer desk mates with my favorite person in the class was enough to pierce straight through my soul. I had wrapped up part of my identity in my little best friend. I followed her, whether I knew it or not, and that was presumably detrimental to my individuality.

Several weeks later, school photo day arrived. The winter months had breezed in, and we had all switched to warmer uniforms. I wore a charcoal-gray jumper over a light pink checkered, long-sleeve collared shirt. I hated my drab gray dress. It covered too much of the happy pink shirt. That combination reflected my glum feelings about school. Mom had brushed my hair and feathered my bangs that morning. I looked the part of a good student, but the joy was missing. When it came to my turn, the poor photographer could not get me to smile. I was not amused by his attempts at making me grin. The look on my face in the photo I still have is one I wish I could wipe off and replace with a confident girlish expression. I had a beautiful smile. Instead, my eyes spoke of questioning what right the photographer had to capture my profile. My stare expressed discomfort and uncertainty. Out of all three years of school photos at Beacon Hill, that is the only one my parents managed to save.

6
Baby Sister

"Mommy, is your baby going to be Chinese?"

I suddenly noticed my mother's growing belly about a month or two before my sixth birthday. I knew she was carrying my new brother or sister, but I couldn't understand the biology. More than anything, I was interested in how my new sibling would appear outside the womb. Living in Hong Kong, I knew the baby's life originated in our new environment, not where we had come from. Every member of my family had flown here from America, and that made us American. I felt as though I needed to know what to expect. I needed my parents to correct me if I was wrong, because I couldn't fit the pieces together in my five-year-old brain. I wasn't interested with where babies came from, how my mother got pregnant, or how she was going to deliver. I was concerned with whether the baby inside her was actually Chinese. My mind was genuinely perplexed over the issue of identity.

My mom laughed at my inquiry. I felt a twinge of embarrassment. Her lighthearted chuckle was answer enough that she thought the idea silly and quite absurd.

Anna was born on my sixth birthday, August 26. Mom had decided to induce since her due date had come and gone.

Induction happening no further than my birthday seemed as good a date as any. Mom was used to going full term or even past forty weeks and thought it would be fun to see if she could combine two of her children's birthdays. Five kids meant a lot of birthdays to celebrate. I'm not sure I would have done any different had I been in her shoes.

At the hospital, it wasn't hard to tell my new sister apart from all the other newborns in the nursery. God gave us a nine-pound, redheaded, pasty-white baby girl who I thought really "matched" me, kind of like a twin, only six years apart. Seeing Anna's physical features confirmed I'd had nothing to worry about. In my mind, her genetic coloring proved she was not Chinese; she was inherently one of us. My heart needed no other explanation.

God blessed my mom with what she considered to be the best hospital ever out of all her OB-GYN experiences. She commented on that fact often, and I knew whatever it was about that particular facility, "Anna's hospital," it meant a lot to her. Anytime we happened to drive by, Mom would always point out the building to the rest of us in remembrance. I can only imagine how blessed and comforted my mother must have felt there, bringing a new baby into a world in which she had only just begun to settle.

Making room for a new sibling felt totally natural given how large our family already was. Sharing my birthday didn't always prove to be my favorite way to celebrate, but on the other hand, it wasn't the worst either. My little light had to figure out how to shine in harmony with another taking center stage. Shared birthdays became the new normal at the end of August and didn't bother me until I got into my upper teens. At that point Anna was a high-energy, pre-adolescent extrovert who enjoyed basking in the spotlight. I suppose she had to earn her place in the family, and her personality made the job easy.

For our birthdays Mom drew ballooned letters and numbers on construction paper, hanging them on the walls around the dining room table. She used a rectangular metal sheet pan for the cake. Cream-colored icing spread evenly over the top set the stage for colored candles ablaze with flickering light. Ceiling lights were turned off for the Happy Birthday song. Friends squished around the birthday kid, all eyes gazing at the cake. Parties at our home were simple but always special. Mine began to feel crowded with not only the growing number of candles on my cake, but more signs, more friends in attendance, and gifts all around. Rather than feeling more important, I began feeling smaller, less seen among others vying for attention.

It wasn't surprising to me that the Chinese people adored my baby sister's cheeks and red curls. They would reach out to touch her bright, wispy top or say something in Cantonese as we passed by, always assuming we had no clue what they were saying. Red, a traditionally favorite color, offset by pure white skin and blue eyes, drew instant admiration of everyone in sight.

Dad endearingly nicknamed Anna his "China doll." She was the first Baucum baby born on Chinese soil, and of course, she did look like a doll, just not quite an Asian one! In Hong Kong you could buy upright China dolls whose Barbie-size feet connected to a little stand in an enclosed, clear case. These were meant not so much for child's play but for admiration and decoration. Each thin female figure was adorned in a Chinese costume with a headdress and painted face. From head to toe, the empress-style outfits were colorful and meant to stay on the doll permanently. These were quite the contrast to the original glazed-porcelain China dolls with stuffed cloth bodies made for a child to "dress" with old-fashioned Western clothes.

It was not hard to love my baby sister, as much as she stole all the spotlight my siblings and I may have previously enjoyed. She had adorable chubby cheeks and limbs, earning the nicknames Chubby Cubby and Anna Banana. We Baucum children, her nearest and dearest comrades, affectionately labeled her with those two terms. She was a celebrity, one who decided to make her appearance after we all had set the scene. Her only job was to walk into a room and bask in the welcoming glory of her fans, all six of us, plus the community at large.

As I began to understand that babies first grow inside mothers, are physically seen for the first time in a hospital, then come home to live, my view on the meaning of family took shape. Adding babies to the family became a normal part of the fabric of life in the Baucum household. At a young age, I had no reason to fret over this learned aspect. My mom kept her personal struggles concealed from us kids. I would have never understood how difficult it was to be pregnant so soon after arriving in a foreign country, so far from home and familiar medical care. There were already four of us clamoring for her and Dad's attention. We were settled in our new apartment home with the routine of life and school. Ministry had been established, but a pregnancy changes everything for the woman who's carrying. Mom had been attending language school part-time while Dad was a full-time student. I had no clue what going back to studying after being done with school in Tennessee was like for them. It would have been a huge relief to complete four years of seminary. Just three years later they were back at it again, with a fifth newborn in the mix.

I have an old photo of my dad sitting in his small, cramped

study with metal-rimmed headphones on, going over Cantonese lessons. He spent many hours in that spare room, which was also used for laundry. In the picture, you can see a dull green washer-and-dryer set on a shelf between him and the doorway. As our family's endless laundry tumbled round and round, he played and replayed lessons in order to memorize tonal words, phrases, and sentence structures. It took a great deal of dedication to keep up with the pace at the language school. After having her baby, my mom acquired a private language tutor at home.

Since Anna was born overseas, and a furlough was not going to happen for another two years, my parents decided Mom should take a short trip back to Texas. Taking Anna back would allow for the grandparents on both sides to meet the newest Baucum baby. It was a blessing that they lived in the same town—a mere three blocks from one another. Ross was chosen to be Mom's travel companion and helper since he was the eldest. Life went on as usual for me while Mom, Ross, and Anna were away. Timmy and Ruth were by my side. Dad was there to care for us. It must have been a big sacrifice for my parents, but important enough. Judging from old photos of their trip, they had a very memorable time.

Back in his cramped office, my dad sat down at his chunky typewriter to write our news to everybody else. "Everybody else" included supporting churches he had personally visited all across America, close friends, individual supporters, and other extended family. His fingers intimately acquainted with the keyboard, he hammered out a line as the rolled carriage eased along to the left, zinging back in place with a ding. The mechanical machine was resolute in receiving imprints of the continuing message. Daddy was always (and still is) the sole news announcer. He loves the written word. His fun sense of humor comes out in his honest, straightforward writing. Crafting family newsletters kept him connected to his community on the other side of the ocean.

More baby additions would be announced one by one over the years. I never read Dad's letters until I was in my upper teens. By then it wasn't uncommon for him to ask my opinion on his writing. As a child I never thought about whether I was in the family news. My name just showed up. Within the first couple of years in Hong Kong, Dad's updates shared how my siblings and I seemed to be adjusting well. I'm grateful many faithful friends read Dad's words in years gone by, praying for the Baucum family. He always expressed thanks to the Lord and for everyone's prayers.

What defined me most in those days was not my dad's descriptive words on a page, my birth order, where I lived, or my lifestyle, but to a greater extent, the confines of my immediate family. That molded my personality and character more than anything. My family was the seat of my security. Everything hinged on a healthy sense of belonging in that central location. Extended family almost felt irrelevant. All the other places that "hosted" me for large portions of my time played a part in shaping who I was and would become, but at the end of the day, family stability is what grounded me.

Occasionally my dad would get the itch to find someplace fun, somewhere we could spread out, away from the cramped city. One day, we packed for an outing at the beach. It started out a glorious Saturday morning. The tide was out, and miniature crustaceans skittled across the smooth sand, their lives interrupted by firm, rounded heels and scores of toes pounding toward the shoreline only to be swallowed up in the balmy water. Dad had driven us and a few of our kid friends out to a remote location in our white Toyota "bread" van, following a winding road around low hills, well past the crowds of beachgoers. We all anticipated a day of sunshine, adventure, and laughter.

Dad was an explorer at heart, eager to see what could be found around each bend off the beaten path. He was also a swimmer, deciding he would swim laps well beyond the shallow end where we children played and splashed that day. At other beaches, lifeguards worked shifts while a boundary net in the water kept swimmers like my dad from going too far. Big red balls bobbed along the rope, a visible signal for people to swim within the limits.

Maybe no one had told my parents what type of marine life swam along the coastline in the South China Sea. Maybe Mom and Dad hadn't heard or taken the time to look up how tremendously diverse and abundant the ecosystem was in those waters. Maybe when my dad swam off, he and my mom remained oblivious and happy, simply enjoying a secluded family outing together. My father's long, strong arms swung one over the other, crashing rhythmically into the easy current, his big hands thrusting back gallons of salty sea. He wore no goggles, nothing but swim shorts.

Within reach on that carefree day lurked a danger that threatened to dislodge the stability that kept my world together. Something long, silent, and ghost-like was floating within those deeper waters, and the strongest person in my family was about to get the shock of his life.

7
Dear Friends

There was no way of knowing what species of jellyfish wrapped its glassy tentacles around my dad's torso, but his body was flaming red as he lay on his back, heaving, barely able to keep his eyes open. All of us had gathered around, looking down on the strongest man in our lives, completely helpless. The heat from the sunshine that morning suddenly felt cruel as it also glared down on my father's stings, adding to the painful neurotoxic burn.

Among the many various venomous creatures that make their abode in Hong Kong, the *Cyanea nozakii*—better known as the ghost jellyfish or the lion's mane—is one of them. It happens to be the world's largest known jellyfish, measuring up to 120 centimeters (more than three feet) wide. This species is responsible for many of the stings that occur in Hong Kong waters, due to its long trailing tentacles.

Dad somehow managed to peel the ghastly barbed stingers off himself and swim back to shore. It was a miracle he didn't drown. I felt scared for him as he collapsed in pain on the sandy beach. What had started out as a beautiful, carefree, happy day quickly transformed into a worrisome, shortened outing as we were all whisked off to seek medical attention. I didn't know the full impact of what it was like to be stung. All I knew was my father was crippled with the agony of what had grabbed hold of him out in the deep sea. Those once friendly waters had turned hostile, forcing a swift departure.

Without a phone or services anywhere in our visible vicinity, my dad had no choice but to force himself to climb into the van and drive to the nearest hospital. That same determination was what brought him back to shore a few moments before. Sheer panic had arisen in my father's mind moments before the sting. What none of us knew at the time, was that while he rested on one of the common, flat, makeshift rafts; a resting spot for swimmers; he caught sight of a swarm of jellyfish. He realized he would have to swim straight through the translucent bloom as no other option of escape presented itself. He eased back in with hopes he'd make it back to his family.

Once at the medical facility, he received much needed care, and recovered.

ON ANOTHER ORDINARY, CAREFREE DAY, MY FAMILY AND I were out on an errand somewhere outside of Mei Foo. There was a steady drizzle as Ruthie and I walked on either side of Mom, the three of us trailing behind Dad and the boys. It was not a main street or a tourist section, just one of the thousands of narrow streets that filled up Kowloon. I have no idea what we were doing that day besides pacing down a random busy street. "Pacing" down any Hong Kong street meant determined, rapid, longer strides. It could easily equal an average day's workout. Fitness centers and gyms were not trending back then, as the majority of people in Hong Kong were already slim and getting plenty of cardio in their daily routine.

Little shops lined the street, each with their own blinking lights and sounds spilling out onto the sidewalk, accouterments passersby invariably tuned out as each continued walking toward desired destinations. Street food shops displayed an assortment of fast food, invariably including my all-time favorite: *cheung-fun, yu-dan* (rice noodles with curried fish balls). The plump, light brown fish balls on a single stick were the best to eat like a hot dog on the go. Other local favorites readily available were egg waffles, roasted whole chestnuts, deep-fried pig intestine, stinky tofu, bright yellow egg tarts, and the list went on, with sweet and salty umami fragrances enticing potential customers walking by. Oversize aluminum lids covering some of the foods were quickly lifted, allowing trapped clouds of steam to rush out and envelope the buyer's path. Gone, even if just for a split second, was all the smoggy street and gutter stench. Present, even if briefly, were hunger cravings too strong to ignore.

Other shops displayed vibrant colors of fresh tropical fruits. Scores of brown, woven shopping baskets hung inside to make room for stacked, plastic tubs, essential homeware and an endless number of knickknacks beckoning to all who trod by. Magazine stands ran the latest issues, invariably dotted with a few explicit images splashed on front covers. I didn't know what that day's errand was about. I only knew it was an ordinary day in Hong Kong, and I was tagging along as usual.

Just past dusk, high-rises pressed in, narrowing our path as we approached a street that was little more than an alley. Even as a small child, I had kept up with Mom's pace, but in one instant I chose to hold back from crossing that street, and I let go of my mother's hand. I'm not sure why our hands unclasped; I must have been distracted, or perhaps my instincts picked up on something. Before I knew it, Mom and Ruthie were already halfway across the road, and I was still standing there, unsure and unsteady in my own ability to decide when to cross the street on my own. Something may have reminded me that what appeared ordinary, even friendly, could potentially be threatening or hostile. So I held back. In that moment, I was untethered, independent, disastrously unprepared.

In that part of the world at that time, pedestrians constantly moved about everywhere with the flow of sidewalk traffic. Jaywalking was normal and usually sudden. People had as much right-of-way as any vehicle on the road. Everyone looked out for any type of movement, whether on foot, vehicle, bicycle, or the occasional hawker pushing a cart of goods. Even with the British enforcing traffic laws, it was normal to experience many close calls, and that was just a way of life.

As I stepped forward to catch up with my mom and sister, clearly aware that was the correct choice to make, a car turned the corner and rolled toward me. We connected at its bumper; the tip of my shoe run over by the driver's tire. I was knocked down to the ground immediately, even as the driver slammed on his brakes, and my foot jerked free. Rain continued spitting from the sky. My mother turned and witnessed what just happened.

There I sat in the street, as though some bully had pushed me over. My knee was bleeding, rainwater trickling a bloody path along my shin. I noticed its course moving down to my right plastic shoe pressed flat at the toes. The driver opened the car door and got out; headlights blazed to a halt. Other people stopped, perusing the scene of the accident. The pause button on life had just been pressed. All in the immediate area could see that the driver had hit a foreign child, a little girl with red hair, her family gathering around in consternation.

I stared in dismay at my pretty new red shoes. I had coveted those shoes, and now one was smushed beyond repair—so very disappointing. Why the tire missed my toes, I'll never know. My toe bones should have been crushed beyond repair as well, but there was no harm whatsoever to my foot.

One stranger moved in close to speak gently with my mother, catching my attention. She was a kind Chinese woman speaking English, attempting to help us. I sat on the grimy, wet ground with a bloody leg as she asked if she should call for help. Mom consented, and the woman scurried toward a nearby pay phone. The other onlookers meant nothing to me; they may as well have been invisible. Only the nice lady who made the effort to resolve our plight struck a chord in me. What would I say to her now, reflecting back? *Thank you! You saved the day. Who are you and why did you stop to help? You have no idea how much that meant.*

Before I knew it, an ambulance arrived, and I was carried inside. I must have blacked out from the trauma because the next thing I knew, I was lying in the hospital, peering up at the ceiling, wondering why the light was so dim, and then noticing all the talkative medics hovering over me. My mother was nowhere in sight.

They seemed to be having a jolly time tending to my injuries. I did not understand what they were saying among themselves, my brain tired from the day's events. Their enjoyment confused me. I had come through a distressing episode, yet here they stood busily stitching up my poor knee, laughing and chatting as if I wasn't even real. I felt alone and frightened. I thought they ought to be working somberly and seriously, not joking around. Of course, I did not say anything, nor was I asked anything in English. I just wanted my mom. I wished they understood how much I needed her close, but only fear slid up beside me.

I left the hospital that night with only a few stitches. What was supposed to be a routine shopping excursion turned out to be another scary incident much like my dad's at the beach—danger intersecting to hurt us—but we were both mercifully spared from what could have been much worse.

Ordinary days turning tumultuous came to a climax one day when my brothers and I were walking through Mei Foo on our usual way home from school. Someone caught up to me and tried to shield my eyes from a horrific scene, which we could hardly avoid since it had occurred in front of the building adjacent to ours. It could have been my older brothers trying to protect me, instructing me to turn and look away. Of course, that just made me want to see what was going on. Little children aren't supposed to look at things that might scare them. Though I didn't get a glimpse of much, I understood that a woman had fallen from a higher apartment and her body had splattered right there on the hard ground. The twenty-story height of those apartments was staggering. Only clothes hung out windows on bamboo sticks, not people.

Dad wrote home about this very sad incident. "Dear friends," he began. "Just as I sat down to write this prayer letter a few moments ago, I heard a loud explosion and several screams. I looked out my window to see a woman lying in a pool of blood. It was obvious the woman had plunged to her death from anywhere from ten to twenty stories above our apartment here in Mei Foo."

Based on the date of the letter, I know I was only five years old. I had walked a safe distance from the scary scene. The next day we had to go to school again, and we were curious to see if there were any signs of the accident remaining. *How do I remember this?* I wonder. *And why?* It was not a personal tragedy. My parents had not left the news on to see if there would be information and details about the investigation of the incident. I don't recall overhearing any discussion among our English-speaking neighbors. My family and I simply were faced with the knowledge of a horrific death in our neighborhood.

We lived among hundreds of people within view of our apartment. Windows stretched up and down the side of each building. Some open. Some shut. Things fell out of windows sometimes, but not people. *Why had that nameless woman fallen? Was she pushed out?* I couldn't help but think about it.

I knew nothing whatsoever about suicide or the fact that jumping from a height was one of the most common suicide methods for females at that time in Hong Kong. I felt sad for the person now crushed and gone. I didn't think about heaven or hell, her eternity at all. Those windows, though. They let in sunshine and breezes. They let us see out into our world. What was God teaching me, so young and naive, new to the harsh pressures of life all around me? Did that scene, the episode I walked beside, change me? Did it give me more compassion for the Chinese people, for people in general? Why the window, the one thing that drew me to its side that first day in our new apartment home?

Dad continued his writing: "Right now, they are cleaning up any visible trace of the tragedy that has just taken place. I suppose it is very human for us to try to forget as quickly and painlessly as possible that death is real and inevitable and, without Christ, hopeless. I hope that I will not forget. I hope that you, my fellow laborers in the Gospel, will not forget. The harvest is white unto harvest; let us not allow it to rot in the fields."

Obviously, Dad saw his lesson from the day's events. A truly impactful lesson, no doubt, for a brand-new, young missionary. I shudder to think that he witnessed the horrible end of that woman's life from his window. But God knew where he had placed us. He knew my family wouldn't be able to reach into every home, every hurting soul in need of real light and love. Yet there we were, right in the middle, experiencing our own personal safety scares as well as seeing in real time the fatal acts of others.

8
Mum

"It's 'Mom,' not 'Mum.'" My mother corrected me again. "Oh, yeah, sorry!" I replied with a grin. She smiled back. Apparently, I had unconsciously switched to a British accent with some of my vocabulary. Attending a predominantly British-run school had that effect on young American students. There were plenty of references at school to our mothers and parents in general, so I quickly adapted to the vernacular.

Even though I attended three full years at an international school, I had zero formal training in the local language or Chinese culture. I guess "international" meant inclusive of every other nationality but exclusive to where we were actually located. My opportunity to pick up one of the most difficult languages in the world was lost during my time spent at Beacon Hill. In that era, my school was not interested in helping integrate the English-speaking youth into the country and culture in which we resided. Instead of learning unique age-appropriate cultural facts, songs, and traditions of Hong Kong and its surrounding region, I was taught Western pop classics like "Yellow Submarine" and other trending Beatles songs. An English nursery rhyme played over and over in my mind once I learned its catchy lingo: "It's raining, it's pouring, the old man is snoring. He went upstairs and bumped his head and couldn't get up in the morning." My favorite jingle that also confused me was, "Sticks and stones may break my bones, but words will never hurt me."

Looking back, I wonder what it would have been like to be submerged into the local Chinese schools from the start of life in Hong Kong. I would have learned how to read and write in Cantonese—one skill at which I never excelled. I would have been far superior and more confident in my conversational speaking level than what actually transpired throughout my years in the city. Parents do what they feel is best and often go with their current options. All the missionary families around us seemed to be doing the same thing. Children were ushered off for a Western education so parents could focus on studying the language in order to reach people.

Apart from most of my week spent at school, I spent much of my free time at a neighboring missionary's home. Their flat was set up like a mini-Americana wonderland. Entering their space was like stepping outside of Hong Kong and into the United States. For me it was as though I walked through a portal that took me back there. They provided a warm atmosphere for all the children, and I always felt at ease and happily entertained. I got my first go at Atari, the early home video game system. I watched the new and original Star Wars movies and fell in love with the cast. I saw scores of old Westerns and other '70s and early '80s movies about roller-skating, flower girls, and even a flying *Condorman*. A closet in the living room housed dozens of bulky VHS tapes. I always wondered how our friends collected so many. A secret dollhouse maze built inside the coffee table fascinated me. Timmy played LEGO® bricks with his buddy, an only son. The older Barnard girls made up games that whisked me off into magical lands of imagination and adventure. Time spent there was pure delight.

I was also introduced, or perhaps reintroduced, to American food I didn't know existed. Food had fun names like Sloppy Joes. Everything we ate was all-American and pure comfort food. There was nothing I didn't like about the Barnards' home.

My mom, on the other hand, enlisted the culinary help of a local lady she'd befriended. Yui Fun showed my mom how every dish, except for rice, can be cooked in a wok. She went shopping for us at the wet market and cooked Canton-style meals. Mom liked fish, so Yui Fun would often steam up a fresh catch of the day with head and tail attached. It grossed us out when our cook suckled on the eyeballs, then mouth-dropped the discarded inedible balls right in the open beside her bowl. Burping aloud and wiping her hands or mouth on the hanging tablecloth clashed with our sense of learned dining etiquette. Her manners felt like child's play, but we soon figured out that they were perfectly acceptable and even encouraged in Hong Kong. This newfound cultural allowance greatly pleased my brothers but my mother had the final say at our table. When our cook was not present, Mom would reprimand her boys when they would belch and subsequently laugh aloud. Dad's boyish sense of humor didn't help her aim at making gentlemen out of them, so it was never completely curbed. For the young males in the family, it was always a contest over who could let out the loudest and longest burps.

No part of the meat, bone, vegetable, or whatever was used in meal preparation would go to waste. Anything set in the center of a round Chinese dinner table always had something beneficial to one's health. Yui Fun served up deliciously salty stir-fried or flavorful steamed dishes. Bland vegetables were never a part of the menu. Clear, brothy winter melon soups became a favorite. We Baucum children developed a lifelong addiction to sticky white jasmine rice and soy sauce. It was not uncommon to discover a pool of light soy sauce at the bottom of a child's finished bowl of rice.

Instead of an aunt or a grandmother, I got to hang out with a hired cook. As I got older, I would linger in the tiny kitchen with our well-seasoned, unmarried helper. With her heavily accented but fluent English, she taught me that good cooks always clean up as they work. They do not let dirty dishes stack up in the sink. They wash and put away as they accumulate. They also take pride in their responsibilities and enjoy the fruit of their labor as they share what they have produced with those who are seated around the table. Yui Fun displayed personal pleasure in sharing her abilities and knowledge with my family. She appeared odd and uncivilized in some ways, but I learned practical life skills that contributed to a strong work ethic my parents also lived by.

As time passed, I would try to remember what America felt like. It felt dreamy. Yet I knew there was something concrete in the recesses of my memory bank: a porch swing, me running down a hallway, the affection of my grandmother. Still, nothing ever quite clear. Old ties were all but cut off outside of my grandparents and the knowledge of a few aunts and uncles in my former American life. My tribe was here with me. With the separation from the US, and all the people and places it held for me, came a stronger attachment to my immediate family and the individuals my parents welcomed into our lives in Hong Kong. The ever-expanding group of individuals I traversed with on the far east side of the globe became my support system.

I got excited when my grandparents came for a short visit. I enjoyed simple activities like going to the grocery store with my mom and granny. On one such trip, I noticed during checkout that my granny had a hard time opening the very thin, pressed plastic bags to load up our groceries. I assumed little tasks like that may be different from what she was used to, so I reached out to help her. I had no idea plastic bags had just been introduced in American grocery stores. My granny was still used to bagging her groceries in brown paper sacks. Little things that might be quickly forgotten and dismissed from other minds somehow hold on in my mind, and I wonder why.

Another day, we took my grandparents across the border to get a glimpse of what was then considered "Red China." Mak was our trusty guide, and as usual he brought along his camera. My understanding of what Hong Kong meant in comparison to the rest of the great land belonging to the Chinese began with that trip, then expanded slowly as I grew up. It was not just another Shanghai. Hong Kong was special and unique. I gave little thought to the differences for most of my youth, but there would be one occasion that would thrust open my view of what "China" meant politically, socioeconomically, culturally, and spiritually. I was the daughter of a missionary, not a diplomat, but the realities on the other side of our border would reveal why we had gone to live in that part of the world.

Having relatives on our turf for the first time stirred my mind to think about how my new residence looked and felt so different for someone else coming here—the place I'd already become accustomed to. Neither of my grandparents divulged their personal feelings about Hong Kong or what they thought of us living there, at least not to me. I was only a child. I was the one who went to bed so the adults could stay up and talk without little ears listening.

Besides a tourist trip to the border, we enjoyed riding on

the red double-decker buses. I didn't know those buses were unique to England and that the rest of China did not have or use them. To me they looked like enlarged playthings. Climbing inside to ride felt surreal, like the inside of a giant toy bus. Our seats on top at the front facing windows provided the most drama. The bus swayed like a palm tree as the driver turned corners and always came to an alarmingly close halt behind every preceding bus. The oversize vehicles were literally inches apart, and I never knew why the driver would want to be that close. I suppose it may not have felt dangerous to the drivers or others on board. People were used to living in absence of personal space. Rubbing shoulders or screeching to a halt were never considered rude or wrong, just part of an everyday commute. As the bus moved along, the adrenaline kept pumping and the adventures continued.

In the '80s, I knew nothing of the plush air-conditioned buses that were destined to take over Hong Kong by the '90s and beyond. Hard seats would soon be exchanged for wider, cushioned ones. I got to experience the stuffy heat inside the old buses with the only relief coming from open windows. But I was just a kid then. No worries over hard seats or the sauna-like experience. Mothers often fanned their children's heads and necks as they dozed, little drooling mouths gaping on shoulders or laps. To keep from being bored, I amused myself by watching adults fall asleep, their heads nodding lower and lower, suddenly jerking up, then back to nodding with the lull of the bus's engine. Sleepy heads swayed easily to the left or the right, almost banging into the passenger sitting rigidly beside them, who would inevitably be awake, trying to mind his or her own business. They sat there visibly annoyed when it got worse, and they would try scooting over, but it was nearly impossible on a crowded bus. Standing for a long ride wasn't ideal either. Their faces showed how much they hoped that the napping stranger would not completely fall onto their neck or lap or, better yet, that they would get off the bus at the next stop. I found it hard not to stare or giggle.

What I did not know was that the routine of my own personal heart-pumping journey was about to dramatically change course. Familiar people and surroundings in my life were about to be swept away, and it began one day with a simple question posed by my parents.

9
New Territories

"How would you kids feel about changing schools?"

My ears perked; my head swung upright. I silently and deliberately clamped down on the phrase "changing schools." Looking around first at my brothers and sisters, then straight back at my parents, I searched their faces for some kind of interpretation.

What did that even mean? I'd never changed schools before. I had no idea what that felt or looked like. In an instant, the image of Timmy's special pillow tucked under his arm flashed across my mind's eye.

After several moments of stunned silence, a barrage of questions and comments began flying out of my brothers' mouths. I couldn't keep up. I didn't know what to ask. I was caught up in a hairy and mostly blurry conversation as one thought broke free only to begin pressing, then squeezing the air from my lungs. I couldn't muster the strength to say anything. Instead, my newfound anguish clung to me as my parents took control of the discussion.

"That's right," Dad was saying. "The new missionary family we just met is opening a Christian school."

"It would be much smaller and different from what y'all are used to," he explained.

"This is a big decision because you know Dad's been looking for a new house closer to Butterfly Bay, where our new church is located," Mom chimed in. "We want each of you to think about it. It might not be easy to leave Beacon Hill *and* Mei Foo." After a slight pause, she continued. "Faith, you haven't said anything. How do you feel about it?"

Mom and Dad were genuinely interested in my feelings about major changes they were contemplating for our family. They wanted us kids to understand the moves we would soon make. It was reassuring that I would not be caught off guard. My opinion mattered to them, though at first I had a hard time voicing it.

"What about Amy?" I asked hesitantly. "Is she going to move schools too?" I had a sinking feeling in the pit of my stomach that I would have to say good-bye to my best friend. I would be leaving her behind—or was it the other way around? The daily interaction, sharing our lives in and around home and school, and the occasional sleepovers would all come to a halt if I voted in favor of the move. She was an important piece in my life that I wanted to hold on to. *Could she change schools with us?* I wondered. It was not to be. My parents confirmed Amy's family was staying; it was just going to be us.

I thought about how it would not be hard to say good-bye to my class, my teachers, or to my school as a whole. But that place provided my most prized friendship. Walking away from that would certainly leave a gaping hole in my world. The resolution was soon made. My siblings and I would not be returning to Beacon Hill.

Only a few months prior, we had met a new missionary family. Not a big deal since lots of missionaries lived in Hong Kong. Privately, they had shared their vision with my parents. They were preparing to open a small Christian school and invited my parents to come on board. It had a strong appeal, but Mom and Dad were gracious to first consider our feelings about it.

Beacon Hill was not what my parents wanted for us long-term. They were not comfortable with the philosophies of education we were getting there. My older brothers were getting a healthy dose of Darwin's theory of evolution in their classes. I was immersed in classic fairy tales. Mom and Dad didn't want their offspring adapting to and possibly accepting a secular worldview over a biblical one. I knew we were in Hong Kong for a particular reason, though I didn't contemplate that reason too much. It wasn't until years later I could see the vision and the purpose-driven life they believed God had for us as a family, not just the two of them as a couple. We were not separate entities from the Baucum family. We were in Hong Kong as missionary kids to minister alongside our parents. Every child was viewed as a key player in my parents' eyes, and this was their chance to raise like-minded youth as much as was in their power to do so. A Christian school would reinforce their values, uphold theology, and encourage Christian living.

What had brewed anxiety in my heart and mind was eventually dissolved to little more than an afterthought. The excitement of becoming acquainted with the new missionary family overcame my feelings of loss. They had three daughters—one younger, two older than me. They were good-natured young ladies who favored each of us Baucum kids. It turned out to be a fair exchange, but occasionally I would think of Amy and my friends at Mei Foo, wishing for the next visit or interaction we might have somewhere.

Our new school was housed upstairs in an office building. School dramatically shrunk from what we were used to. The

Baucum children doubled the size of the entire student body, making it a grand total of eight! We walked away from the enormity of Beacon Hill to a family-sized, family-run institution. From laborious roll calls to time-consuming counting of heads waiting in lines, we now had only four new classmates to consider. My one and only known world of academia was instantly swept away into a compilation of memories.

After house hunting for several weeks, my dad discovered a newly built, much smaller apartment complex in the developing New Territories, several miles outside the hustle and bustle of Kowloon. The location was key. He needed to be closer to the town of Tuen Mun. He also did not want us to be too distant from a daily commute to our new school. Castle Peak Villas offered just the spot. It sat halfway between both church and school and far enough away from the city smog.

Castle Peak was drastically different from Mei Foo. We moved from a first-floor flat among twenty-story skyscrapers clustered all around us to the fifth floor of a nine-story building. There were only ten apartment buildings in the small complex, all centered around a wide-open concrete courtyard with a sunny playground. From there we discovered easy access to an undeveloped, overgrown, rocky shoreline that provided countless hours of exploration.

Besides searching for and moving our family to our new home, my dad went through a lengthy process to achieve consultations with the government in order to secure the church plant location. Since the mission board that we were under was a private organization, he was allowed to apply in their name. He had to simultaneously figure out the finances and decide on a community service plan for the building as well as partner with a local seminary student who would be the main translator, associate pastor, and eventually senior pastor. Dad was going full throttle, and all I can remember was my angst over leaving my best friend.

Once we had settled into our new home, summer holiday was coming to an end, and we had to figure out the fifteen-mile commute to school every day. We no longer had convenient school transportation. There was no one to pick us up. How would four kids, the eldest only a preteen, navigate their way back to a small inner-city office building on time five days a week? Fifteen miles may not seem like much in other places, but in Hong Kong, it's a complex web of highways, narrow streets, railway lines, and all the double-decker and mini-bus lines including trams interconnecting Kowloon, Hong Kong Island, the developed districts on other islands, and growing towns throughout the New Territories.

It was up to the four of us to cocoon ourselves out of depending on cushy private transportation and blaze our own trail through the maze of our city's public transportation system along with the majority of the other five million residents. The trip felt as though it took half a day each way. We had to take a long bus ride and then a shorter train ride. My dad must have given proper directions and escorted us at first, but I only remember my brothers leading. In that time and place, child endangerment was not really a focus, and it was deemed safe to come and go without constant parental supervision.

Boarding a bus in Hong Kong was simple, as long as correct, or close to correct, change was prepared while waiting in line at the bus stop. That was the only method of paying the fare. In our hands we clutched currency that bore the image of the queen of England. Her youthful minted portrait became very familiar as much as Abraham Lincoln's bronze profile becomes familiar to any kid growing up in the United

States. I liked the queen's appearance on those coins. I thought she looked pretty with her delicate features and plated crown.

We also needed individual plastic train cards to swipe ourselves through the main concourse, then jump on the escalator headed downstairs to the underground Mass Transit Railway (MTR). The card was needed again to leave at arrival, so if little hands lost one, it made the trip that much more complicated. Each MTR station had color-coded tiled walls with English signs for directions. Many of the station names were in English, which allowed expats like us to ignore the Chinese words and follow what we knew.

I always felt a strong adrenaline rush each time I stood on the MTR platform watching a departing train pick up speed, window pane after identical window pane flying by. Snapshots of passengers willingly held hostage were carried away within the illuminated cars that were crowded at first, then sparsely filled at the ends. The rushing metro forged on, undeterred, unapologetically sucking in blasts of cool underground air with it, swooping my skirt off my knees as it bid farewell. In a split second, the train thundered off into the deep, pitch-black darkness of the looming tunnel. Oncoming trains appeared from out of the darkness on the opposite end, headlights glowing, charging forward to rescue all of the awaiting passengers. As it pulled in for a rapid arrival, its force pressed me back another step on the unpretentious platform.

One day during our hustle and bustle of boarding, I turned around as the sliding doors swooshed shut and saw one of my brothers still standing on the platform outside the train. The doors provided a tight hold on those of us safely inside, barring all else out. There he stood, alone, staring back at us. Each of us three on board were not any less bewildered than the other. As the train began sliding forward, he began walking alongside the platform, unsure what else to do. We all felt utterly helpless in that moment. The reality of what just happened sunk in with dread and loss. The four of us were separated. But we were supposed to stay together! We needed to stay together! What was he thinking? Why hadn't he paid closer attention and run into the train with the rest of us? Three of us watched our brother wave his arms toward the front end, where the conductor would be able to see that he missed a passenger. It was a futile attempt at flagging the train down. Our day had just become a lot more complicated.

Another incident occurred when my sister accidentally dropped several school books into the space between the platform and the subway. To me those few inches felt like a gaping gorge ready to swallow up anyone who wasn't careful getting on or off the train. Our textbooks were not heavy, but rather slim paperbacks. It happened as Ruthie cried out about the books slipping from her hands. We turned around only to peer down the darkened chasm, questioning what actually happened. In a flash, we exited the train and watched it leave without us so we could identify the missing items. Sure enough, they lay dejected far below, images on the covers swept up in a slight breeze. We knew they were needed the next day for school. What would Mom and Dad say? Would they be mad? We blamed one another for being so clumsy and not helping our little sister. Once again, our day just became a lot more complicated.

Besides those skirmishes, the four of us made it a whole year unscathed—never even realizing the process of commuting together in such a manner was bonding us. I was unaware that my siblings and I were living an adventurous life, learning things most American kids our ages could not fathom doing on an ordinary day. Yet there we were, on that side of the planet, going with the flow, rubbing shoulders with Hong Kong's masses on a daily basis.

If public transportation trips felt long, rides in private vehicles could feel just as long. Dad drove us back and forth to church along a coastal highway. Many who did not take the underground railway, which only went out to a very limited section of the New Territories back in the '80s, had to use that highway. All the buses and taxis traversed on that route as well. Because of the high volume of vehicles, we often sat in traffic jams. Windows stayed wide open, leaving my whole family completely exposed to any onlookers from all the other vehicles passing by. For some reason, I felt the looks from people when in the van but not on public transport. I knew the locals would be surprised to see a whole family of foreigners, mainly when we were in the New Territories, far outside of the expatriate bubble of Kowloon and Hong Kong Island. This was not easy for me, even though I was used to living in Hong Kong. Their looks of surprise or stares reminded me that I was different. I was not one of them, and I ultimately belonged to another country. Regardless of how comfortable I got with my life, my outward difference would always define me.

Moving to a new school and a new home birthed a year of change. My loyalties once strongly attached to my friends at Mei Foo, Witness Church, even my school, had to unravel. Where I belonged was so much more than a house or location, a close friendship or a group I felt a part of. People of different nationalities came in and out of my life. Every new scene of my journey would provide its own set of friends and community, and it was my job to learn to adapt, to give of myself as well as to receive. The time would come for my family and me to return to the United States, and that would also stir the cocktail of identity and belonging inside me.

10
Butterfly Bay

By 1985 my family was fully engaged with the outreach ministry of Butterfly Bay Baptist Church and its cooperating Elderly Center. The church's location was surrounded by several large housing developments within the town of Tuen Mun. The facility was aboveground on the first floor of the centralized community center, providing many residents an easy walk to and from their flats for a variety of respectable social services. The six-story building was designed with handicap accessibility conveniences, a spacious auditorium, and an oddly placed palm tree in a lifeless courtyard.

In the early days, my parents taught English as a second language to generate attention and interest in the church ministry. The Elderly Center received immediate participation, while Sunday services began from scratch with little to no community engagement. Flyers for church and evening language classes were posted and spread around the area. My dad used the opportunity to freely weave the gospel message into English lessons. There was always a draw for business-minded individuals or the younger generation to learn English, especially with authentic American or British teachers. The local schools taught basic English grammar and vocabulary, but few students comfortably spoke much more than "Hello, my name is . . ."

That brings me to Brother Luke. Luke was the new seminary recruit—dirt-poor, single, and full of smiles with a love for serving the Lord. Dad took Luke under his wing, and he soon became my dad's right-hand man. Butterfly Bay and Luke became one and the same in my mind. One was incomplete without the other.

I once went with my father to visit the young man at his home. Before that visit, I had never seen poverty with my own eyes. I did not know people could actually live in shacks and shanties. This was an area of Hong Kong that was not built up with skyscrapers or littered with shops and restaurants. Each "home" was held together with tarps, metal slats, and an assortment of materials you could probably find in a garbage heap or landfill. I couldn't believe my eyes. We lived like kings and queens in comparison. I knew I was expected to be polite and use my manners, so I withheld my shock at the knowledge that this friend of the family was actually living there.

In my mind Luke was not defined by his economic status. He was just Luke. He played guitar, enjoyed singing, appeared pleased to be in long-term partnership with my family, and exhibited a vitality in ministry. Like Mak and the other young adults from Witness, his life intersected with ours, and he entered into genuine friendship with my family. He chose to walk and grow with us. Luke was an unlikely, unassuming Chinese man who assisted my dad in the first church-plant undertaking.

Since my father was the founder of the Elderly Center, he enjoyed attending their social events and made every effort to personally greet the seniors who joined in membership. He did not lead their events, as Chinese social workers were employed to manage all the activities and events.

At one Lunar New Year's banquet, my dad took us kids with him to the hosting restaurant so we could greet each table with a cheery "Gong Hei Fat Choy!" (or "Happy New Year!"). Children provided an extra level of pleasure to the older generation who were celebrating the biggest Chinese holiday of the year. In his arms my dad carried two-year-old Anna, while the rest of us followed him. All of a sudden the already boisterous restaurant atmosphere ramped up in volume as the seniors noticed my dad holding his chubby-cheeked, red-pigtailed daughter, greeting them all with the traditional well-wishing phrase. They simultaneously began extending their personal stashes of *lai see* (red envelopes) at arm's length for my father to take, fiercely insisting he take them for his kids. Much to Dad's amazement and embarrassment, he tried refusing politely but was overcome by the mob and could not have them losing face over his misunderstanding of culture. My family had not yet been this closely exposed to the symbolism of the long-established form of New Year gift giving.

Every one of the elderly guests commonly carried around red envelopes stuffed with brand-new, crisp bills through the entire lunar holiday. The tradition was for married couples or elders to happily give to their children or grandchildren, nieces and nephews, and younger family friends who all took time for courteous family visits. The excitement was in opening each envelope to discover how much money was inside. The closer you were in relation, the more you received, typically depending on the giver's financial status.

In years to come I would excitedly draw in my breath in hopes of receiving lai see from generous married couples and acquaintances. As foreigners, my parents were not expected to hand out red envelopes, but they adapted to the custom and still enjoy giving in this manner on special occasions.

At one of my favorite nonholiday large gathering events back at the Elderly Center, we participated with the staff in handing out goodie bags. All the seniors sat on padded, burgundy, metal fold-up chairs in the auditorium. Those were not sturdy, plush-padded seats. They were thinly lined, skinny metal chairs meant to hold smaller people. In general, southern Chinese elderly folk may have been a bit overweight, but never obese. After a variety of speeches, awards, and entertainment on stage, including the Baucum children singing a song or two in both English and memorized Cantonese, we would help hand out the gift bags. When we sang, we stood there sweetly and obediently, boys taller in back, girls in dresses up front, looking much like the von Trapp children in *The Sound of Music*.

Toward the closing, I eagerly seized as many bags as my hands could handle. I was always excited to walk the rows, and deposit treats into aged hands of grateful guests. It was a satisfying feeling to serve those ancient, wise souls. I don't know what the giveaway contents included besides mandarin oranges, but it was the same idea as children's birthday party loot bags. My siblings and I were the most popular distributors on the planet judging by the smiles on the recipients' faces.

Those senior citizens might have gotten a kick out of seeing cute American kids politely participating and helping at their community event, but I know they helped me too. The opportunity to be a part of something bigger than myself helped to shape my values. Grandparent figures in my life were almost nonexistent up until that point, and though a major language barrier still existed between us, those people lit up my life. I did not know how much I needed them to love on me, to accept me for who I was, abiding in their world, but that is just what they did. It forever shaped the way I viewed the older generation. I was young, there to serve people who had lived long lives, their physical youth shrouded in a cloak of gray, white, and wrinkled, weathered skin.

I'm so grateful for simple ministry tasks my parents gave us kids to do. They were activities that intertwined ministry and community service. Being given the opportunity to be involved in both was a wonderful gift. The seeds planted from those early positive experiences grew into a desire to volunteer in all sorts of community programs and church ministries over the course of my life. I have always seen myself as an able volunteer for things that help and nourish people.

At age thirty-seven many years later, I got to visit Butterfly Bay with my husband, my son, and my parents. We stopped by the center on a weekday to look around. As we walked toward the main entrance, we came up behind a woman, stooped with age, slowly making her way up the steps. In stunned amazement, I recognized her, wondering if my eyes were deceiving me. My mom joined me, and we immediately greeted her in Cantonese. I wanted to know how old she was. *How in the world could this woman still be alive?* I wondered. She said she was in her nineties and was glad to see us again.

I regarded the encounter as a direct gift from God that day. What a delightful surprise to show up on a random day to find a lady who was still getting herself out and over to the place she'd been a part of for three decades. A small but indispensable place, special to both of us.

THE YEAR MY FAMILY AND I WERE SCHEDULED TO RETURN TO the United States dawned. It was 1986, and we had arrived at a predetermined time to leave the field and do what missionaries do: reconnect with family and the home church, update supporting churches in person, rest and recoup from the stresses and pressures of life as "active duty" foreign missionary workers. Most missionary parents typically wanted their own kids to get back to seeing, feeling, and knowing firsthand what it was like in their home country, among their own countrymen. The farther away they were from the home culture and lifestyle, the more the parents saw the need for a furlough. My parents thought along these lines, no different from the other missionary families I knew.

Butterfly Bay Baptist Church was growing with a small but healthy core membership, many of whom were young people, a couple of families, and some elderly folk. Luke was going to be taking on the senior leadership role while my dad was away. With the anticipation of our upcoming trip came the knowledge that we would be going back to a place and people I hardly remembered. My grandparents on my dad's side were most familiar, especially since they had visited us in Hong Kong. I tried hard to bring up memories and locations, relatives, and our church in Amarillo, Texas, where we would soon return for an entire year—the year I would turn nine. I do not remember looking at photos that would help me refresh my memory of forgotten names and faces. I guess it was expected that kids would do just fine, no matter how long the absence.

Four years of my life meant two apartment homes, two church families, a new sister, two schools, a best friend, friends of all ages from a variety of nationalities, new front teeth, a new scar from stitches on my knee. I was taller, had doubled my age, had thicker hair, had more interests and knowledge of the world, was now somewhat bilingual, a third culture kid, and an international traveler. What I didn't realize before our big trip was how much I had melded nicely into Hong Kong's building-stacked, upward-growing, high-volume flow. My family and I were growing much like our city of residence. A new sibling equaled an additional bed, another seat at the table and in the family van, more birthday celebrations, more toys, more clutter, but best of all, another playmate.

My dad planned and purchased seven international round-trip plane tickets: two adults, five children. I've always wondered how in the world my dad could make a single purchase for plane tickets whether it was seven, eight, nine, or finally ten people total. In all of my growing up, including my teen years, I never saw the actual total amount my parents spent on getting our family across the ocean. I don't recall seeing a bill or a statement for it or even so much as hearing a complaint from either of them. As a kid, it never occurred to me to think about the price tag of that many international airline tickets. Why would I when my parents didn't bring it up?

Before the internet and online purchasing, Dad spoke on the phone with travel agents. He would discuss the route we needed and all pertinent travel information. It was always a very important phone call or two. After some years passed, he got connected with a Christian travel agent he trusted and used each time we headed overseas. Her English was great. She was efficient, working quickly to get us what we needed, for the best possible price. Dad never seemed to miss a beat at getting everything squared away for upcoming family trips. There were so many details to figure out, besides making the purchases necessary to get us all back to Texas. My parents made sure we kids knew how we needed to pray, asking God to provide a vehicle and a house to live in while Stateside. Those were always the two big needs placed on the forefront of our minds.

Sitting comfortably on our first return Boeing flight over the

Pacific, my siblings and I made friends with a couple of young adult Chinese ladies. They took to us kids quickly, and we were soon engaged in what felt like hours of silly card games. A photo was snapped as we sat scrunched in the same row, cards in hand, big smiles, shining eyes. Those ladies felt like the other young adults we knew, loved, and missed back at Witness. They had the same friendly delight in us children, and we soaked it up. Energy flowed back and forth between us and our newfound friends, making my trip back to the States memorable and fun.

Upon disembarking at last from the final connection, we scurried along with heavy carry-on bags through the bare jetway. The short tunnel wasn't meant to be anything but quick access to get passengers and crew out of the plane and into the airport terminal. But it meant going in reverse for me. I'd gone this route forward, away from this original place. My parents were bringing me back to a place called home, but the only home I knew was what I'd just left behind. I carried a concoction of places and people full of meaning with me—places and people inscribed upon my heart, just as real as if someone had tucked a little pillow under my arm with identifying names stitched all over. Names like Mak, Patti, Luke, Serena, Yui Fun, Reverend Loong and the group of elderly folks at Butterfly Bay, Amy, the Barnards, dozens of classmates, even Mrs. Stout. They had all changed me in ways I couldn't comprehend in my youthfulness.

The open door off the jetway moved closer and closer. Taller, shuffling bodies blocked my view. An interior light pulled me forward. Each person stepped toward it and melted away into the wide-open room at the gate. Then it was my turn, and I looked up to see a sight I never could have pictured.

11
Texas

INSTEAD OF BLINDLY FOLLOWING THE EXITING PASSENGERS and the guidance from airport employees, I fastened my eyes on a cluster of people staring right back at me. I recognized my grandparents positioned in the center. Smiles lit their faces like candles on a cake. My family members moved with me as one force toward the front-facing group, a group that held signs and began waving. Recognition dispelled intimidation, and like mosquitoes to bare skin, we met a barrage of hugs. Everybody circled around us right there at the gate. The encounter was immediate, up close and personal.

We had returned from what most called the mission field, but to me it was just home. After traveling halfway around the world, we converged with an intact community anticipating a reunion I didn't know I was invited to. I landed in a place I'd altogether forgotten. The previous four years had swallowed up memories of America, yet not in such a way that made things look strange. I felt a certain familiarity in returning. Nothing I saw struck me as severely as when I first entered Hong Kong, but still, there were a lot of people besides my grandparents who magically knew us.

"Hi," one of the several kids who had gathered around me spoke up, as I stood there, observing the commotion.

"Hi," I said in return.

"Welcome back!" the girl said.

"Thanks."

And that was all, but it was enough. That simple acknowledgment, mingled with the reception I was witnessing, filled me up like a warm bowl of Yui Fun's nourishing winter melon soup. The feeling absorbed through my skin, making its way through the fibers of my being, reaching into my soul, filling me with a sense of gratification. But wait. Hadn't this same scenario happened when we first arrived at our home in Mei Foo? Parents with kids my age came to welcome us, while at first I kept my distance near the living room window, so unsure of what it all meant to be in Hong Kong. We were received as though everything was totally normal.

This welcoming party was different because all these people already knew me by name, liked me, drew me in as though I were one of them all along. What I soon learned was that these people were among our biggest fans. They prayed for us, they read my father's newsletters, they placed their own money in the offering plate to support what we were doing far away.

Going back to where we started from was like putting the gears in reverse, except I hadn't known what reverse felt like until I stood face-to-face with a Texas welcome. All the experiences I had had were instantaneously minimized in order to be fully present. The quintessential mission field felt much too far away, far beyond the present, yet I still had its scent on my clothes, its taste on my breath, its sensation within my heart.

I quickly settled into my place among the church kids and their families. It was as though I'd been with this group of kids all along. We ran up and down the church halls together, passing along whispered messages of who likes who. Our cheeks flushed with the after-service thrill of parents lingering in conversation, leaving us free to roam and play.

In the first weeks and months of that year back "home," it was nice to feel loved and embraced for who we were. Lots of people already knew my family and I. But did they really know us? They hadn't walked crowded streets, run to catch the bus or train, or lived in a high-rise. They'd probably never walked through a smelly, wet market with bloody, freshly butchered meat hanging on hooks, ready for purchase, with foreign currency, in a different language, of course. I didn't even have the words to describe my life over there. My dad could, but I had no thought of doing so until we showed up at a supporting church. All of a sudden, we were put on a pedestal and introduced as "very important, real, live" missionaries, and all the other little children should sit still to hear what we had to say and to hear us sing for them. My dad showed slides that clicked along narrated by his good-natured voice. Even then, the projected scenes on the screen felt like a lifetime ago.

That summer I was old enough to attend junior camp. I was thrilled to go. The boys and girls had made me feel at home, and I enjoyed backcountry cabin life with them in the Rocky Mountains for a whole week.

In the fall I was enrolled in the church's private Christian school. That was great, but placement testing required I go down a grade. My academic level was not where it should have been, according to their standards, and it gravely disappointed me. The kids I'd attached to were all going into the fourth grade, but I was relegated to third. The year began. The door to the classroom I had hoped to be in looked as though it were a mile away on the other side of the gymnasium. The kids in my class were slightly younger than I was, which was fine. I resolved to fit in as best I could. Coincidentally, one of my classmates was a missionary kid from the Philippines. The kids made fun of her at lunchtime because she apparently enjoyed "eating bones." She was odd, but so was I. I just didn't have any strange habits that everyone noticed. I knew she had lived in a faraway place that even I could not picture. I couldn't even muster up enough imagination to know what her day-to-day life looked like back there. Of course she was different. Years spent in a completely different world will change anyone. The other, "regular" children didn't have parents who had taken them to live anywhere peculiar.

It felt like the people in our American community lived by a different standard of time altogether. The routine of school life was good and steady, but outside of that, there was no rat race, no hurry up and walk or drive fast. Looking around town, my biggest wonder was where all the people were. Did everyone stay inside their house all day? How come there weren't any pedestrians on the streets or families filling up the beautiful grassy parks? The wind blew tumbleweeds wistfully across the road. I got the sense that time stood still in Amarillo. The city displayed an astronomical downsize in traffic and total population from what I was used to. At first I didn't miss it. It was soothing to the ears to hear fewer sounds and noises. It was nice to hear all English and not have to work at interpreting in my head. Strangers didn't look my way. We looked like everyone around us, so there was never the surprise in someone's eyes when any of us showed up. When we drove alongside another vehicle, no one turned to notice and point, mouthing the word, "Gweilo."

My family and I enjoyed crispy fried-chicken dinners from my granny's oven. Aunts and uncles gathered with us at times for the meals. I wondered why none of them had kids. On a few occasions, we enjoyed dining out at family restaurants. We scarfed up big, juicy hamburgers and steaks, crispy Texas toast, aluminum-lined baked potatoes dripping in butter and sour cream, sugary fruit pies, all while downing plenty of Dr. Pepper in ice-packed glasses. I learned that food portions and everything else is bigger in Texas!

My father acquired an eight-passenger Suburban with no air conditioning, so we drove with windows down, mesmerized by the wide-open, crystal-clear blue skies, no skyscrapers to block our view. We went to spacious parks shaded with large oak and elm trees and swung high on playground swings. My siblings and I were each other's playmates. Our favorite outdoor spot was my paternal grandparents' well-groomed front lawn. We rolled around and spun cartwheels in the thick, soft grass and frolicked in the sun. Green grass was a luxury for kids from a concrete jungle.

My grandparents worked hard to make that year unforgettable. Ruth got a piñata—first time for a Baucum birthday. Granny, my dad's mom, organized fun party games and hid real quarters for surprises in our birthday cakes. At Christmas our toes combed through her dark moss shag carpet in the den as we gathered around cherry-red and emerald-green wrapped presents of all shapes and sizes spilling out from under the tree. In place of hanging stockings, she set us kids down with construction paper, scissors, glue, glitter, and buttons for us to decorate our own large brown paper bags, which she'd saved from her trips to the grocery store. Each of us made our own; then we lined them up in front of the fireplace.

In the spring, Granny pulled out her fine china for girly tea parties. We got to dress up in floppy sunhats and her old gowns. At her ladies' sorority luncheon, we girls sang "In the Sweet By and By" with my mom. My other granny, Mom's mom, taught us to love flour tortillas warmed right over a gas stove, rolled up in smothered butter and honey. Her cheese enchilada and Spanish rice dinners were to die for. I had not become acquainted with the goodness and satisfaction of Mexican food before this first trip back to Texas.

I began to feel very "American." I no longer had to try to imagine what it was like to live in America. I would always remember now. I would not forget the faces of loved ones and friends. I would remember the kindness extended to me and bottle up all the warm and fuzzy feelings. Going back to Hong Kong would not be so shocking. I knew what we would be going back to. I finally understood that I was an American returning to live in an Asian country. It wouldn't have to shake me so much or change me further. In my heart I believed in myself. I believed in my family. My family made up the strongest pillar in my life. Their presence reminded me that I was safe, I was loved, and that's all that mattered. I could move and settle with them anywhere.

My confidence was building that year, but would it be enough to withstand more changes, some rather unwanted changes?

Shortly before getting on the return flight, my sisters and I learned that Dad and Mom had decided we girls would not be wearing pants anymore, except for occasional "necessary" activities such as horseback rides, snow days, and some sports. They had met other families outside of our home church who lived by that dress code standard. They thought it would be best for us as well. What might have seemed like a minor change was huge for me.

I did not like the idea, but it was non-negotiable. I loved my jeans; they were comfortable and I even felt more Western in them. I knew mine were not as cute as some styles other girls wore to school. I had noticed theirs had denim bows attached to the lower back ankle. I had never paid attention to jeans before then. But this was a firm decision my parents had made. Pants were relegated to be worn by boys and men.

While I had no problem wearing skirts and dresses, outward appearance mattered more to me than I realized. It wasn't about the need to be more feminine. It was about my identity being back in the States. The ease at blending in felt good. If outward appearance was one of the ways of retaining that feeling, then stripping away a part of that left me vexed. I cringed at the new rule that affected me just because I was a girl. My brothers got a free pass. I suppose it would have helped my attitude if I had been taken on a fun shopping trip for new clothes to make up for my loss. All I did was slump down against the wall in the dining room.

What is meant for good in Christian homes, sometimes unintentionally leaves room for legalism to get its foot in at the door, smiling slyly in its undetected reach for power and control.

A tear-filled good-bye followed back at the airport, luggage bursting at the seams, checked and carried off to ride in the belly of the aircraft. Almost identical to the way my family had been greeted upon our arrival in Texas, we discovered an excited group of people on the other side holding signs and waving as we entered the Arrivals Hall in Hong Kong. Brother Luke, who'd taken over for my dad when we were away, led an assortment of young and old people I immediately recognized, along with some new faces. My father was overjoyed to see his young partner in ministry having stood strong for the duration of our furlough.

Although I felt much more American at that point, my place was really on both sides of the ocean. Even if I favored one dwelling place over the other, I would have to learn that settling in to both, one after the other, was going to have to work.

Our new house post-furlough was even further out in the New Territories. We moved into a Western, suburban-style neighborhood called Fairview Park. It had been built a decade earlier in the Yuen Long District by a Canadian Overseas Development. Our church was nearby, so we would not need to drive along the busy coastal highway to get there. Our new home was designed for a single family. No one lived above us, and no one lived below us. We even had our own small yard and driveway! At the time, it felt spacious by Hong Kong standards.

What would being uprooted and transplanted again do to the flourishing young lady I was supposed to become? I couldn't tell what was happening below the surface. I only saw the tangible. It was like the porcelain China doll standing gracefully inside one of the glass display cupboards in our new living room. The landlord left it there for us to admire, or perhaps it was a good luck charm? I wanted to touch her delicate features, and when I did, a piece broke off. I did not dare confess to my parents. I did not want them to have to pay for it, nor did I want to face any type of retribution. Instead, I carefully set the piece back as though nothing had happened. But I knew something had cracked and she was no longer perfect. I knew she was damaged, but I had no way to fix her on my own.

Something like that was happening inside me as well. The blame could be placed on continual changes, roots unable to sink deep, fluid environments, or the impact of the variety of cultures on a naive soul. It could also point to conflict I was witnessing within the confines of our home. Conflict that had no name. The truth was, we were all dealing with inner imperfections and unseen forces that sought to pull us apart. Adding law-driven requirements to our lifestyle simply to appear more spiritual was something my parents recognized later on and with grace and humility, stepped away from.

As days turned into months at our new house, my parents broke the news that Mom was expecting baby number six. The Baucum family, and my place in it, was about to be stretched and refitted all over again. God was in the midst of writing a script I could not see. He was fashioning a story that would connect our small ministry with a greater work he had already begun across China. The script was unfinished. Would we collide or ride with the movement of his hand?

12
Deeper Waters

A GENTLE SEA BREEZE BRUSHED MY THICK HAIR OVER MY shoulders. I squinted from the bright sunshine as I looked around, first at several leisurely beachgoers, then back at a group gathered under a makeshift tarp flapping in the wind. I sat alone on a large rock a few feet away. A couple dozen church attenders sat nearby listening intently to my dad preaching in English, followed by Luke's immediate translation, line by line. The two of them sounded rhythmic as they worked their way in harmony through the mini sermon. Luke was an excellent translator. My dad needed only to prepare messages in English, knowing his associate pastor was capable of interpreting accurately.

That day was baptism Sunday. With no baptistry in the building, we all made our way down to the nearby beach at Butterfly Bay. It wasn't white sand or crystal-clear water, but there was more than enough depth to immerse anyone who was willing and ready to take that next step as a follower of Christ.

Why wasn't I brave enough to be baptized back in Texas? I thought to myself. A nice inside baptistry was positioned behind the pulpit and choir loft. I had watched other kids take the plunge, but I was too timid to step forward in my faith. I had learned it was supposed to be done out of obedience. When I told my parents I was ready after growing up a little in Hong Kong, I hadn't thought about the experience taking place out in the open for anyone to watch. I'd only gotten scared from hearing a sermon about hell, knew I didn't want to go there, and silently prayed for Jesus to save me again, just in case. My parents never pushed me but taught me that following in believer's baptism was the right thing to do.

My sister Ruth had decided as well. She and I were the youngest in the group of about ten people. Sitting there under the full sun, I was not eager for the sermon to be over. I waited patiently, feeling qualms about wading out into the deep, exposed to the public. Everyone else appeared excited for this day. I had nothing to lose in comparison to them. I later learned in bits and pieces how some of the Chinese believers were risking everything with their decision to follow their new Lord and Savior. Buddhist families were not happy, and some ostracized the Christian son or daughter outright. Others had come to salvation after generations before had prayed for such a day to dawn. I got to witness a tiny part of a fascinating spiritual work that was taking place before my eyes, except there was no real comprehension on my part. I was just one of the six preacher's kids, and ready or not, I was there for the ride.

My father was visibly pleased to lead me lovingly out into the South China Sea. Luke had me by the other hand. Like the story of Peter in the Bible, I couldn't help but notice the choppy water slapping waves against my body. But fear did not drive me down. I let two people I trusted firmly grip my arms and lower me backward until I was fully immersed in the balmy water. I came up, soaking, to see giant smiles, and my turn was done. I didn't feel any sort of transformation or hallelujah song, but I'd made a volitional move that would set my sights on trusting the One who would keep a hold on me through even deeper waters ahead.

~

Hong Kong had two channels for English-speaking residents and visitors: Asia Television (ATV) and Television Broadcast Limited (TVB Pearl). One day a big news story caught my attention. I don't know if my parents wanted me to watch and see what was going on in the world, or if I was drawn in out of my own interest and curiosity. But there I was, mesmerized by what the screen was showing. Just beyond our city, out into the great expanse of China, a civil war was being waged. The headlines swept my mind away from my home to a far-off, yet not-so-far-away city called Beijing.

Young adult Chinese students were out protesting their government. Tanks rolled toward them in objection, wielding the power of the Communist Party. Individuals, fearless and weaponless, stood their ground directly in front of the armored vehicles. It did not seem fair or good; the logic did not add up. The news reel that day became my classroom, my lesson in government, history, geography, warfare, and civil unrest.

Tiananmen Square was way up north in China's capital city. To me, the location of the battle felt as unrelated as any other surrounding country in Asia. Hong Kong had its own land mass carved out from a larger and unfamiliar land called China. The populace in my city were known to be cultured, open to the rest of the world, protected by the Crown, living their lives freely. Just beyond the border lived a separate, larger group of Chinese people, run by a vastly different authority.

The world watched what communism looked like in real time. I watched what communism looked like, far outside my world yet so close. The thin frame of one infamous student who stood his ground facing the oncoming tank showed us, young and old, what the fight for liberty meant. It meant everything.

At eleven years old, I could not define the word *communism*, but I could see that it clearly stood for something. After viewing the news that day, I did not need a lecture on democracy or types of government around the world. All I needed were those few glimpses of ordinary, unarmed civilians demanding freedom while their own government openly refused. I was one of many Hong Kong residents of all ages and backgrounds impacted by the events up north on June 4, 1989.

It was around that time I got the idea of writing in a mini notebook. Current events revealed a harsh brevity of life. Like those students, I had something to voice, just not out loud. At first it was silly, meaningless tidbits about daily occurrences. My writing eventually morphed into journals providing an outlet for my swirling emotions. I had become uneasy with my appearance, unsure of how to relate to anyone as I was entering adolescence, and unable to clearly communicate any of that to my parents or anyone else. My heart cried out to sit with my mother, longing to hear words of comfort, to have her untangle the emotional knots. But my feet would not take me to her. Instead, I kept the usual pace, striding in motion with the orbiting world around me.

The Bible I'd grown up with beckoned for me to open its pages, urging me to discover my Shepherd who longed to take me by the hand; to lead beside still waters. Journaling helped me to express myself with pen and paper, the silent speech maker. My journals, paired with the Psalms, became my lifeline. I would feel a pull toward both. As I unloaded onto the page, my written language sharpened. When one book filled with words, I went on to another freshly purchased, pretty one—a clean slate on which to inscribe my thoughts. My ever-changing world felt more stable after seeing it laid out on the page. The significance of my Christian foundation and worldview kept weaving throughout my musings and offering a place for my spirit to rest. Remarkably, I've kept all those journals from my youth. Scattered pieces of years past fill up a deep gray storage bin along with other keepsake items. An entry or two caught my eye as I browsed through well-preserved pages recently, reminding me that I was never once left alone. Choosing gratitude, joy, forgiveness, and hope forged in me a determination to be whatever it was God wanted me to be.

At age eleven every Hong Kong resident had to get an identification card. It didn't matter what nationality you were or what passport you carried. The ID basically showed that you had the right of abode in Hong Kong and were not an illegal immigrant. I felt grown up when I got my first card. It was white and laminated with my picture and personal ID number. I would show this card at the airport when flying back into Hong Kong. The card itself showed who I was in relation to my city of residence. It meant nothing while residing in the United States. What was important and necessary in one country was of no value in another.

Carrying a HKID card not only identified me as Faith Baucum, but it also gave me the assurance of a rightful position and legal standing in my local Chinese community. In my other hand, I carried an American passport that identified me as an American citizen with all the rights and privileges of international travel. Planting roots felt possible, even necessary, while I lived in Hong Kong. I had begun thinking like the

Chinese as my conversational language skills increased. But would my security and ability to communicate be enough to see me through the inevitable changes Hong Kong itself was rapidly heading toward? The needed pieces to my puzzle were about to be tossed out as my family and I continued in motion with no expectation of ending our ministry there.

13
Ebb and Flow

"Bohhhhh-beeeeee!"

A firmly emphasized, two-syllable word frequently bellowed from the neighbor's upstairs window. It was actually the English name of their white mutt, a fiercely territorial male. Bobby would bark at anyone who came too close to his owner's gate or tried entering the house. A sharp order in Cantonese usually followed. I always thought the girls yelled his name best. They spoke in a commanding voice with just the right descending stair-step tones, and the guard dog got the message to quit making a fuss.

Chan Wing Yat and Chan Wing Yee were sisters who lived next door. They were about the same age as Ruth and I. They also had two older brothers as well as a grandmother, all of whom stayed out of sight. The girls enjoyed coming over to the side fence in the front yard to chat with me and Ruth. In the beginning we four sisters taught each other new phrases to communicate better. I enjoyed our informal conversational language classes with my new friends.

The family next door was apparently wealthy, though I had never thought about what wealth looked like other than what I saw on television. The high-value component to my neighbor's property seemed to give them a false sense of superiority. In the driveway sat a black Mercedes-Benz. The luxury vehicle received the utmost care from the head of household. I often saw the girls' dad single-handedly washing and waxing his car under a shady tree. He was not a driver for some company, as he wore no cap or uniform when he left. The cherished item received attention and care not afforded to any other on the premises. A status symbol, before I knew what that meant, closely maintained by an enamored owner. Every nook and notch were tenderly wiped and polished. The inside was cared for as well, never a smudge or bit of clutter seen through the clean windows.

Almost daily, we children would go out to ride our bikes or play games on the narrow street. If the Mercedes happened to be parked at the sidewalk, all of us quickly learned not to go near it. My friends punctured the fun time we were after with an emphatic command offered more as a stern warning—"Doen touch my Fa-da-cah!"—but lacking any reprimand if disobeyed. We took it as somewhat comical. We obeyed, much like the dog, but also chuckled at the absurdity of it. We were not out to destroy or bring damage to our neighbor's prized vehicle. I knew it wasn't about that. Any swipe or imprint of a child's fingerprint might cause the girls to get in big trouble. They guarded their father's property like hawks. I felt sorry for the daughters of such a man. They were loyal to him, but I wondered if he was as interested in his kids as he was in his car.

By all accounts, my neighbors were living the ideal Hong Kong dream life, if there ever was one. With his big, gated Western-style house and guard dog, the fancy car owner could afford to have more than two kids, provide them with a good education, and care dutifully for his aging parent. Materialism at its peak. Those were the families everyone else envied and strove to become. Every dollar saved for the kids, if only to see the offspring enjoy life like that. The culture of the day encouraged education and making as much money as was earthly possible. It reflected in the city's structural planning, though time was not in their favor.

In October of 1989, the governor of Hong Kong announced that a decision had been made on a long-term development strategy. The plan was to construct a completely new, world-class international airport. The glory days of Kai Tak International Airport, the place that first struck a cognizant chord in me, would come to an end within the next decade. The leaders of the city I lived in were not interested in slowing down their momentous stride forward. Before my time, Hong Kong had once been identified as nothing more than an assortment of poor fishing villages. I resided in a metropolis recognized as one of the most developed cities on the planet, exploding with international trade and commerce. I recall the buzz over trying to beat the clock and open the new airport before the 1997 handover of Hong Kong from the United Kingdom to the People's Republic of China. It did not open until the following year, but the incredible feat remains one of the biggest operations ever seen in aviation history as well as the most expensive of all existing projects of air hubs, as listed in the Guinness Book of World Records.

Entrepreneurial expansion, free enterprise, and pro-democracy media outlets were also sailing toward an expiration date. The 156-year British rule was drawing to a close, returning sovereignty back to China. My family and I witnessed an exodus out of Hong Kong. It seemed justifiable after the Tiananmen Square Massacre. Hoping for a better financial future, as well as looking to dwell under a governance like the one they had been brought up under, families split up, sending one or two members to study abroad long-term. Others who could afford to leave left as a family unit, often connecting with relatives in various parts of the world. Some of the previous generations carried memories of courageously fleeing the mainland during Mao's Cultural Revolution in the 1960s and '70s or returning along with a tide of refugees after the Japanese occupation in the 1940s, attempting to live peaceably in Hong Kong. I was living through a small segment of the significant and historical ebb and flow of migration solely based on political upheaval.

In the meantime, my dad partnered with an organization to get new American missionary families *into* mainland China as English teachers. At times, he would escort them so that he could make contact with the institutions where they would be working as well as to explore the province. He continued planting churches in Hong Kong, and my family participated in a variety of mission work as well as trips back to the States. Furloughs coincided with new babies, though all four of my younger siblings made their first appearances in Hong Kong hospitals. In the '90s, I focused on activities I enjoyed, like sewing, crafts, baking, earning money on the side from tutoring and bake sales. The great land of China remained distant and, excluding its ancient history, totally uninteresting in my opinion. I viewed the mainland as backward, its citizens lacking real understanding of how the civilized world operated and deprived of accurate knowledge of their own history.

On one occasion, Tim, Ruth, Anna, and I had the opportunity to go visit a missionary family across the border. They had kids and teens our ages, and it was not far. I enjoyed our visit and easily noticed differences between where they served versus where we served just a short distance away. The American family poured their hearts into the people they were ministering to, the majority students and common folk. The young people typically appeared overjoyed to connect and make friends with Americans who came to live and teach in their region. Missionaries residing on the mainland were careful not to identify as religious figures. They took a more cautious approach to sharing messages from the Bible, as opposed to our open, street-style methods in Hong Kong.

Traffic outside of Hong Kong looked like a horde of rhythmic confusion as everyone weaved their own way through by foot or by wheel, staying alive at the same time. Using bribes to wiggle out of any traffic ticket or having key connections with someone in a position of authority to clear the offense were both as commonplace as rice on the dinner table. The postal service was also not reliable or trusted by foreigners. Before receiving anything, all mail could be opened and potentially confiscated. These were all basic realities I came to learn about not only from taking a trip and seeing for myself but also by hearing reports from my dad and from other families traveling through Hong Kong. Countryside or village folk in China were considered poor peasants, their lives bearing little to no value or dignity in the eyes of others. I also read books that were banned in China, published in the free world, written by people who had grown up under Chairman Mao's regime. Though my generation had not suffered directly under Mao, he was still idolized. While I wouldn't have considered myself extremely studious, I did glean a basic understanding of how some stark societal differences were rooted in China's recent history.

My family was comfortable living in Hong Kong in the mid-1990s (besides never quite adjusting to the ever-present large variety of cockroach and spider). We worked hard to clean up a shell of a house Dad had discovered for rent outside of

Fairview Park, somewhat in the countryside, and it was bigger than all our previous places of residence. On the property grew a healthy lychee fruit tree (a favorite of ours). Grass grew in the backyard space where we tried planting a little garden. Our dog, Peach, brought a litter of puppies into the world, much to our delight. An open, covered garage was used as a temporary carpentry shop as well as a place to hang a basketball hoop. Glorious morning sunlight bathed the dining room each clear day. A large balcony above the kitchen overlooked plots of green vegetable gardens the neighbors grew for the market.

Our family homeschooled, Mom utilizing her big kids for help with the younger ones. We enjoyed cooking and baking together in our large kitchen. We hosted many church youth group activities, short- and long-term visitors, as well as others traveling via Hong Kong. Dad reflected about how he felt this was our permanent home. As long as the landlord didn't want it back, we were there to stay.

It was in that house I celebrated my eighteenth birthday, my parents gifting me with an intricately carved, solid wood hope chest. I was thrilled to be given such a large and beautiful piece of furniture. That chest represented a protected place where each keepsake item would be able to lie still and await a future of which I could dream. Little did I know, God was moving under the exterior of my ideas of how life would go, presenting outrageous directions for my family no one could have expected. My dad sat our family down after returning from one of his routine trips into the mainland, prayerfully and quite delicately spilling the news.

14

Hainan

WE SAT DOWN AS A FAMILY ON OUR WICKER-FRAMED BLUE FLOral couches. I liked those couches. I'd sewn curtains to match. We were used to Dad leading daily family devotions, sharing wisdom from the Proverbs. It would have been strange if Dad didn't have anything important to say. He was the communicator and took seriously his role as head of the home. Everyone else listened. But on this day, my dad had something pressing to share after returning from the province I knew only in name as Hainan.

He described how he had been exploring the island province and had stopped on a country bridge after seeing a large rock inscribed with a unique title: "The Ends of the Earth." He sat on that bridge to listen and determine what God was trying to say to him. He knew of a verse in the book of Acts that talked about bringing salvation to the ends of the earth. He felt the Lord was directing him to be that light among the lost in Hainan province. It wasn't just about sending others anymore. It had become personal. My dad could not ignore the urging he felt to surrender and obey. In the past, he and Mom had surrendered together, as one, not only for their own salvation but for mission work and in choosing a home church and where to attend seminary. This time it was all Dad.

I listened, feeling incredulous. Dad was telling us our time in Hong Kong had basically expired. Our many years growing up, expanding our family, starting churches, writing home about our experiences, was all coming to an end. And we were one year shy of walking through the much-anticipated 1997 Handover! God wanted us to just up and leave? To miss out on the historical, once-in-a-lifetime occasion? To go straight into a country we didn't really like, never wanted to see more than on short visits? What about the brand-new church plant that hadn't even gotten off the ground yet? What about our house we worked so hard to fix up and beautify, and the idea that this was our forever home? What about all the baby Christians who needed my preacher dad? What if it was only me that really didn't want to go? The younger kids were too young to consider other options. Me? I was already eighteen. I could vote and drive in America.

Dad laid his burden before us in hopes that his family would not resist the way he felt God was leading. I do not recall everyone else's emotions upon taking in the news, but I do recall our circumstances. Mom had just buried her own mother back in Texas. She'd made two separate trips to spend precious time with her only remaining parent, who was dying of cancer. My eldest brother was getting ready to go back to the States. He and Tim had already gone back to work for a few months. They were both feeling out what it was they were supposed to do with their lives. Like them, I hadn't yet come up with a plan of my own. None of us really entertained the idea of going to college full-time. Due to strong influence from our homeschool founder's methodology, my parents felt no inclination to usher us older kids off to higher education. It was a "new approach" theme for families—that of raising "arrows" full of inward character, which in turn would be enough for them to conquer whatever they felt called to do.

Ultimately, I knew I was free to choose. I could go back to the States instead. I don't know when exactly I felt like I would stay and proceed forward with my family, but it happened nonetheless. I found myself sorting through belongings, wrapping up final graduation requirements, helping around the house. A close family friend selflessly took it upon himself to pack and ship my hope chest to my grandparents' permanent address. That bit of my life would not be coming with me on the new adventure. It would have to be set aside for an unknown time in my future. Saying good-bye once again to familiar surroundings proved to be seamless for me. But this time, I'd be going not as a child but as an adult, to live in a province I'd never yet stepped foot in. With that token, my dad asked if I'd be interested in teaching English full-time with him at a foreign language school. He had made contact with a woman who operated a nice school in need of foreign teachers. I would be paid as much as he was and any other teacher if I could handle the formal position. He had no doubt I could do it. I had no doubt that if Dad were there alongside, I'd be fine. But *living* in China did not carry much appeal. My discomfort at the idea did not change the first few weeks upon arrival.

I DON'T KNOW WHAT IT IS ABOUT NEW DECISIONS TO FOLLOW Christ, whether as a baby Christian or a well-seasoned one. The decisions seem to prop giant targets for the enemy of our soul to shoot at, bringing doubt and even despair on the part of the decision maker.

After one month of moving into a dank, three-story villa in the capital city, the island was struck with a typhoon, the likes of which we hadn't seen since our earliest days in Hong Kong. The storm wrecked any sense of normalcy. We lost power and running water. Buckets had to be filled and carried over from a nearby pump in order to flush the toilets. I remember wetting my hair at night just so I could cool off enough to sleep under a light, airy sheet. Thankfully, screened windows kept the hordes of mosquitoes at bay. Dry shafts between the ceiling and the floor above us invited who knows how many heavy-duty rats to take shelter. We heard them scurry about. I was used to seeing large insects in Hong Kong, especially once we moved to the country house with the lychee tree. If bugs scared me, big gray long-tailed rats had one hundred times more power to do so. Once the typhoon passed, my little siblings played and splashed in front of the house, thigh high in the flood. I cringed at the filthy water up to my knees as we gathered for a photo.

At first it felt miserable knowing this island city was home for who knew how long. If only I had known how breathtaking the island was beyond the city limits. I did not picture beach vacations in Sanya, the southernmost city, a newly developing tourist spot. I had no idea I would meet and serve literally hundreds of people from all corners of the nation. I did not plan on discovering a heightened level of appreciation and endearing love for the friendships I would attain in the days to come. I had no vision of those we would intersect who had family roots in a strong Bible-believing faith brought by early missionary influence of years past. I had no idea that Chinese food was not limited to Canton-style Chinese food. Each of the provinces had its unique dishes, cooking methods, and flavorful spices that would explode my taste buds, teaching me of the country's incredible diversity that I'd not known up to that point.

Our villa was situated in a cluster of houses only used for businesses that provided their employees free temporary housing. It was included in a worker's salary. Half sat empty or cycled individuals in and out. Directly in front of our place of residence stood an apartment building full of single-child families, the one-child policy strictly in place at the time. Soon enough, my youngest siblings found other little kids to run and play with. At first they interacted in the universal language of children. They quickly and naturally learned basic vocabulary faster than anyone else in the family. Those of us who were in high school and above went to learn Pinyin, the official romanization system for Standard Mandarin Chinese. I learned that Mandarin was not as difficult as expected. It only had four tones that I was able to grasp quite well. It was good to discover that some words were similar to Cantonese ones. We were not about to dive into the much more complicated Hainanese spoken throughout the entire island along with other languages and dialects. It was recommended we stick to Mandarin, as everyone in the cities grew up learning it along with whatever mother tongue they were born into. The past fourteen years spent in Hong Kong gave my family and me an advantageous step ahead of all new missionaries arriving in China. We were already suited for the job, so to speak.

Hainan province was not an independent island, though that would have been special in and of itself. It was China's newest province as of 1988, and it was designated a special economic zone (SEZ) in an effort to increase investment. A gold rush of sorts occurred that lasted through the early '90s. Entrepreneurial expansion, including new businesses and new jobs, brought in people from all parts of China to work, to make money, to push the limits on what the government was allowing. Most were settling right where we did in Haikou, the capital city, but others were moving to establish and work at hotels springing up all along the largely untouched tropical beaches of Sanya. With that activity came the heightened awareness of the need to communicate in English, the global business language. It helped that we as Americans already stood in admiration across the board in the eyes of educated urban dwellers. We were given instant attention and a huge platform on which to showcase our core beliefs. It all came by invitation, absent from the threat of having visas revoked for unlawful religious activity. On that first Christmas, we were asked to stand on a public stage outside a big shopping center to sing English Christmas carols. My dad was given the opportunity to share how and why we celebrated the season. We were featured in newspaper articles and magazines time and again, either individually or collectively, all favorably. We had not known the likes of such celebrity status while residing in Hong Kong.

Our new boss gave simple instructions on what would be required of her new teachers. In that time and place, it did not matter that I had no job experience or college degree. She was just glad to have a third teacher, as it was difficult to find foreign teachers in an out-of-the-way place like Hainan. I flipped through the English "textbook" that was photocopied from a publication out of the United Kingdom. I quickly learned that copyright laws did not apply in our corner of the world. Although I was quite familiar with British pronunciation and vernacular, I was not impressed with the "book." Teaching American English would become the new normal once my dad was able to recommend and send off for the materials we desperately needed. At the start of the first eleven-week course, having labored over how to stretch a one-page lesson into a two-hour time block, my nerves lit like dry grass on a hot west Texas afternoon. The school took in a larger than usual enrollment as advertisements and word of mouth spread quickly: "Learn English from real foreign teachers!"

I had the sense that I was supposed to be there, to do the job well, to simply take one class at a time. I had tutored kids privately throughout my teens. How hard could it be to teach beginners the basics of communication? I was more than used to Chinese people. They did not intimidate me, I reminded myself. I had just celebrated my nineteenth birthday. My age alone would give me more credibility, I assumed; plus, I could act and dress older, I thought. The very first night class would squash all sense of self-reliance, revealing I was in over my head. I had no idea just how naive I was going into this arena.

15
In Over My Head

Heat crept up my neck, flushing my cheeks. It wasn't the weather; it was all nerves. My eyes narrowed, double-checking the notes in the teacher's guidebook as my brain pressed on the internal question of how in the world this same exact lesson didn't look anything like the lesson I used that morning with another group of students. My morning class had gone beautifully well. That group of ten had accepted me happily from the start, and my initial nerves had settled quickly as I melted into the friendly gaze of each one in my class. I was the brand-new teacher for the beginner-level English classes. Tonight was supposed to be a replay of what had transpired that morning. But this evening was not measuring up to the success I'd enjoyed only a few hours earlier.

An uneasiness stirred among the first two rows. These were not fidgety children. Most were much older than myself—professional people, blue-collar workers, college graduates, moms and dads. Who was I? Just an uncredentialed missionary kid, barely out of homeschooled high school, trying to look and sound older as a professional ESL (English as a Second Language) teacher. The only reason I stood up front while all others sat before me was because I was the foreigner in their country. I was an American who had signed a one-year contract with Inter-Foreign Language School; they were Chinese, hungry to learn my mother tongue.

Okay, let's ditch the book, I said to myself. *Let's press play on the DVD lesson while I think of what to do next. This video is easy to follow. It'll get the attention off me for a second. I can't let them see how nervous I feel.* I kept smiling and acting enthusiastic as the video played for the class. It was pretty corny, and it completely derailed the direction I would have liked to take the class that first night of the eleven-week course.

Then she spoke up. Not the lady in the video lesson; the woman in the front row. Her words sounded totally unfamiliar to me. But her tone was clear and universally understood. She was not happy, not one bit! She continued talking louder than the video volume, which was set high for those in the back of the room to be able to hear. Competition ensued. *Let this person keep talking over the video lesson, or crank it up to hush the perturbed student?* I debated within. Others answered her, but nothing was being resolved. Instead, a sharply argumentative debate set in. I had no way of answering the woman's dilemma, and she seemed to be pointing out the obvious fact that I was in over my head. The situation spun out of control while my amygdala kicked into high gear.

What am I supposed to do? I thought. *This lady is forcefully expressing her dissatisfaction to the whole class, unhindered by her emotions. I'm not prepared for this eruption in any way whatsoever, and I have no way of explaining anything with the language barrier between us.* I lamented. Not one soul in the room was able to translate, to intervene, to explain the misunderstanding, to patch things up so we could move on. My enthusiasm and sense of success stemming from victory earlier that day completely vanished. The facade fell, just as she wanted it to, exposing the fact that I was not a real teacher, not qualified, fit, or capable of teaching anything. Clearly, I did not belong in that position.

I stood there, alone, stunned at how chaos had escalated so quickly right before my eyes in the white-walled artless room. The stupid video played, prompting the class to stand. *Stand for what?* I looked back at the screen. It was teaching the word *stand*. Apparently, when you first learn English, you're supposed to know the action verb *stand*. English 101. *No one is following the lesson,* I thought, *and no one cares. Can I dig a hole right below my feet, crawl in, and hide?* My mind pleaded, desperate for an escape. *Can I run away? Will anyone notice if I dash for the door only a few feet from here? This isn't what I signed up for. I can't do this. She is showing it like the light of day in case some others hadn't noticed.* I bewailed my plight.

Just then, a man in the second row stood to his feet without saying a word. He rose just as the video continued prompting with hand motions. *Really?* I thought. He visibly demonstrated cooperation, silently defying the raucous scene, supporting his new failing teacher. He squared his shoulders and looked decidedly to the front of the room. Standing alone among the class of confused students, all apparently strangers to one another and to me, the teacher. The heat that had risen up to my forehead drained just a tad. Tears threatened to fill my eyes, but I refused to let them.

Not in front of everyone, not in this unresolved chaos! This is a language school. These people are paying good money for me to teach them something. I willingly accepted this position. For about two seconds, nothing else mattered. Someone believed in me. Someone understood the madness wasn't about me or my lack of ability to be the teacher. I could do something about the threat I faced. I observed the solo participant with admiration. *Thank you!* My eyes spoke into his. I hadn't even learned his name yet. Would the rest of the class follow and stand with the man, defying the lady's power over them? Would they shift direction, allowing me to attempt getting us back on track for the night?

My hopeful couple of seconds crashed, trampled underfoot. The class remained too unsettled. My hero's attempt at putting an end to the unpleasant situation and promoting cooperation went unnoticed and unappreciated. The majority won. I raised my index finger motioning for the class to hold on and wait while I went to get someone who could help. I let myself out the door, rushed to the front office and into my boss's open door, tears streaming down my face. I sloppily explained what was going on. She immediately grabbed the receptionist, assuring me it would be okay and they would take care of the class. I need not go back in. She knew how to handle her own countrymen and countrywomen.

With gratitude I hastily made my way down to the end of the hall toward the ladies room. I wanted my dad, but he was teaching another class and it would have been foolish to interrupt. The W.C. (water closet, as they called it) offered a row of dimly lit squatter toilets, windows wide open, overlooking a lighted portion of the city I was still unfamiliar with. Retreat from the intimidating woman who'd successfully stolen my opportunity to teach that class allowed for more tears to flow even faster. I should have felt relief, a slowing of my heart rate, but instead, felt a tightening in my chest and throat. My ability to self-regulate stunted. My vision blurred as I stood there crying. Thankful for the twilight shrouding me, hoping no one would come use the bathroom, all I could do was face the window and talk to the only One who knew exactly where I was and why I was all torn up inside. *Why did you bring me here to do something that is way too big for me? What is the point if I can't even do it? They don't want me; they want a real teacher.*

I wrestled with the question of why I had moved with my family to Hainan. It had been Dad's calling. I heard feet shuffling down the hall and turned to look at my face in the mirror. I saw a reflection of a distant memory gazing back at me. An eleven-year-old girl with thick bangs, twice-folded layer of white gauze taped to her chin, insecure, embarrassed. She was the big sister but didn't have a clue how to do grown-up things. She was disappointing everyone.

"Wait up! I'm coming!" I squeaked, wobbly steering my mom's bike around a corner. I had decided to wake up early to join Mom and Dad on their early-morning walks. I'd missed the usual sound of the alarm clock ringing in my parents' bedroom just above me but felt the front door slam shut. I jumped out of bed, dashed to the bathroom, then woke Anna like I'd promised to.

It was just after dawn, but the skies were overcast, making it feel even earlier than six a.m. I heaved my sister up into the mounted child carrier. I enjoyed escorting her around on my mom's bike even though she had long outgrown the rear seat. She crammed her body down and buckled herself in. We were off in a flash, my feet pedaling as fast as they could. I knew the route and eagerly urged myself forward. Mom and Dad heard me call out, turned around, and saw us about thirty feet behind.

After getting their attention, happy to be catching up so soon, I didn't notice the speed bump. In my haste, I had forgotten it was there. Instead of a smooth ascent up and over the bump, my bike launched, then bounced. The handlebars jerked out of my control, twisting the front tire, throwing me entirely off balance. Instead of the usual glide forward, I glided downward with a hard thump. The point of my chin hit the concrete, but I pushed my hands solidly against the road, lifting my head up to catch a glimpse of my parents, now racing toward me and the scene of the accident. They rushed to grab Anna, desperately checking to see if she was all right. I had not thought of my little sister as we both went down. She was not crying, not making any noise or movement. She came to quickly, then began howling from the scrapes she had acquired.

Once Anna was in my father's arms, my bike lifted off the street, we made a beeline for home. We got in the van to go to a nearby hospital. My chin wound required stitches. My sister was patched up with regular bandages, her injuries not as deep. I left with bulky gauze held in place with tape along the bottom of my face.

"Faith, I hope you know the only reason Mom and I went straight for Anna was because she wasn't moving or crying. She's a lot younger, and we were worried she was hurt worse than she was," my dad explained later, lest I entertain the idea that they didn't notice me or care as much as they did for my sister.

"It's okay. I know." My emotions felt awry, much like the front tire I had tried in vain to direct. *The eldest sister inadequate for big jobs,* a deceiving voice whispered in my ear. I listened and allowed my confidence to deflate. Insecurity showed up each time I glanced at myself in the mirror, embarrassed at how I looked like I'd sprouted a white beard.

Those same eyes now pierced into my present, asking what right my nineteen-year-old self had to be in a classroom teaching older adults. Mixed messages from my new surroundings created uncertainty. Why pretend to stand out when in fact I longed to fall back and remain in the shadow of others stronger than myself?

The answer to my inner conflict came at last. A short verse I'd learned from 1 Thessalonians shot into my panicky processes. "Faithful is He that calleth you, who also will do it" (1 Thessalonians 5:24). I mentally grabbed ahold of it, muttering it over and over. I dried my eyes, took a deep breath, and dismissed the bait to quit. God was and had always been faithful to me, to my family. It didn't matter if I couldn't see how in this moment. I had been raised to face the unpredictable scenes of life, to assimilate even in the uncomfortable.

The next day, my boss rearranged for me to teach instead an upper-level beginner class, leaving the Chinese teachers to work with the lowest of the beginners. She apologized profusely, knowing I'd "lost face," but I was grateful I wouldn't have to go back in with the angry, dominating female. I never found out who she was, who the courageous man in the second row was, or any of the others. Perhaps all the characters of the charade had taught me what I needed to learn, right at the start: hit hard from the get-go, then adjust my sail to the steady breeze. That seemed to be the pattern of life for this missionary kid, didn't it?

16
Pieces To My Puzzle

When the calendar arrived at the year and month of Hong Kong's ceremonial Handover back to the People's Republic of China, the event did not feel as important as it did before we'd moved away. That large and looming date no longer carried the same weight. I already lived in China, operating in a world that had gladly taken my family and me in, though we had to tread cautiously with mission work. I continued teaching the eleven-week courses, cycling new students in and out of classrooms with blank white walls. The longer I taught, the better I became at the art of teaching. I had never thought about how frustrating and complicated my mother tongue was before teaching in Hainan. It was my job to present digestible English lessons at the level at which my students came to me.

My biggest blessing was that I never had to inspire anyone to learn in my class. They all wanted it. I was the carrier of the skills they sought as well as the means to an end. I found myself opening up to them, sharing stories of my youth in simple language, almost like speaking to my youngest siblings. Bits of my life were fed to attentive ears, receptive souls. So many of my students had never been outside their country, even to

Hong Kong. With that, I found a childlike wonder and interest in what lifestyles and ideas lay beyond their scope of knowledge. My presence brought a fresh take on what real outsiders looked and felt like, not limited to what they had viewed or been told through censored media channels.

Day after day, night after night, I worked solo in regard to lesson planning and presentation, never once partnering or sharing duties with any others employed at the school. At our foreign language school, though I was either the daughter or sister of some of the other teachers, I was no longer a child, dependent upon or blending in with the strength of my family. My classes were my own responsibility so long as I could manage to relay information.

In the beginning, stress crept into my psyche, eager to dismantle my resolve, my purpose. I understood quickly that I was enormously unprepared and the only way to catch up was in the daily grind of doing the job. Were it not for the practice of mentally going back to my foundation of desiring the presence of the Lord in the privacy of my own heart, I don't know what I'd have done to cope. What would I have turned to? How would I have sought peace and clarity?

I eventually found myself back in the classroom where I had been all but thrown out. The atmosphere bore no resemblance to the original, and I made headway with new students keen on learning. I also developed friendships with many outside of class time. A tribe formed within each group I taught, due to most everyone wanting new friends and better job opportunities that English fluency would provide for them. Meeting after lessons at restaurants and cafés became the norm. Socializing in the "real world" offered another avenue for English practice as well as connections with those who might be interested in moving beyond surface conversations toward deeper discussions.

Conversational English was all the rage, and I gladly disregarded grammar, diving headlong into conversation starters in role play. Though the task of standing before a group of people appeared daunting at first, it helped me grow, allowing me to spread my wings, to see that I had something good and profitable to give. The tension also reminded me that I was ultimately part of a bigger calling, much bigger than myself. I could be a conduit to reach past the surface and pour into the hearts of those I served. The universal humanity I observed taught me that no matter where I live, people have common struggles, desires, needs, and all deserve a chance to thrive.

A few of my lady students told me about their husbands' open unfaithfulness and how crushing it was, all while knowing infidelity with a mistress was not unusual. Those women craved a love that could reach and rescue them from the ugly stains of abandonment and subjugation to an unhappy, though materially blessed, life. I felt a deep loss at seeing their personal struggles. I was faced with the fact that I did not have it in me to fully meet their needs, to fix or satisfy every seeker of English or spiritual understanding. The task exceeded my maturity level, yet fortitude allowed me to continue moving forward each week with everyone who came my way.

One sweet married couple shared how they longed for a second child, but because of the one-child policy, they dared not. They told me privately how they would both lose their jobs and their home as well as receive stiff fines for noncompliance. They understood their government's effort to control population growth, but it did not change their deep desire to grow their family. Still, others could work around the policy, finding ways to have a second or third child. The only way I knew how to console people who shared their personal pain with me was to listen well and show that I cared.

It was not uncommon for someone to tell me I did not seem like the American young women they watched on television or Hollywood movies. I did not dress or talk like them, have the same body language, nor was I a part of the modern family stereotype. As a result, many heard about the basis for my personal belief system.

Hospitality on the home front continued as it had in Hong Kong. Students entered our house and expressed how they felt a difference inside. We upheld morals and traditional family values, all of which they understood and appreciated. Our visible lifestyle resonated well with the majority of our guests. We invited those with improved English and a desire to know more to visit our home specifically on Sundays. My dad shared Bible lessons entirely in English, then later with a translator. We also gave those students copies of the Bible they could read in their own language. It was an honor and privilege to actively participate in providing scriptural answers to difficult questions.

Teaching in a leadership position stretched me in a way I'd never experienced. My naivety evolved into understanding what people were after and how I could promote the common ground we shared. That alone served its purpose to bring out dormant qualities both in myself and in my students. Working full-time in a position of service, I could see God shaping and molding me into what he had planned all along. Moving to the "Ends of the Earth" had been a necessary merge into a people group I hadn't quite seen before, hadn't been interested in previously. Though teaching in China had not originally been of my own pursuit, it was nevertheless an opportunity I stepped into. The great needs I discovered on that island province turned around and provided pieces lacking in the puzzle of my life. It solidified my worth beyond the profile under which I grew up. The weeks and months spent there became a classroom for me, teaching me lessons I may not have learned anywhere else.

After a year and a half, I flew with my family back to the States for my eldest brother's wedding. It was my first time to meet my new sister-in-law. This was to be the pattern for meeting the in-laws for many of us in the years to come. After the celebratory event, my parents hit the road to visit supporters sprinkled around the country. I opted to spend my time partaking in a variety of self-improvement courses and working volunteer positions where I engaged in fulfilling and enjoyable social groups.

By the end of 1998 I faced the decision of whether to stay in America for good or return to China with my family. Again, I knew I was under no obligation to go back. No contract had been signed; no promises had been made. But it was nevertheless a choice I would need to make as a single young woman. The teacher's salary in Hainan was nothing to brag about, but I knew the job carried much more significance than the money it paid. In contemplating the path I would take, I asked the Lord what he wanted from me. My parents would continue on the road God had carved out for them, and until he made it clear they were to stop, they saw no reason not to get on the plane and return to do what they'd done since 1982. I was a third culture young adult, and with that came a strong familiarity with international flying, as though it were nothing more than getting in a car to drive to another state. It was not a giant decision, really. It was much like deciding when to head home for the night. Not much held me down in the States, so I let my parents know I'd join them soon after they left.

Just before arriving back in China, I found out there would be other foreign teachers I could share an apartment with should I be interested in living on my own. The school was increasing our pay, so it would easily cover rent. What I did not foresee was a significant and extraordinary increase in enjoyment I would discover upon befriending a new American teacher from Northern California. She went to work under the Baucum ministry, and the two of us became fast friends, exploring the island together, then taking bigger trips to see more of China. Together we walked the wide expanse of Tiananmen Square, the strangely distant and scary place I'd never dreamed of seeing. Chairman Mao's large portrait hung at the Gate of Heavenly Peace, but my mind held images of young people resisting tyranny, protesting for democracy, never to be memorialized in that place. We flew to Xi'an, home of the unearthed Terracotta Army, intricately carved soldiers for China's first emperor. We met up with former students who were either from those areas or knew them well. They helped us check into hotels, get back and forth from tourist sites, and most importantly, try the local cuisine.

The craziest dining experience was at a famous restaurant. It was famous for a reason beyond my knowledge, and our students knew it would be fun to watch our faces as we observed a certain delicacy set on our table. The waitress presented the "drunken scorpion"—live scorpions climbing a tower of sorts, about a foot in height. The arachnids had been literally doused in alcohol to the point of intoxication, moving about much like people would under the same influence. It was meant to be entertaining as well as a dare to partake. Diners could taste the flavor of the particular beverage used with each crunchy bite, stingers removed. My friends encouraged me to try one, and though I considered myself adventurous about eating unidentified foods, often just to be polite, the mental block was too strong. Even my companions refused to nibble. They ended up asking the waitress to indulge while our faces cringed in observation. I'm afraid we left the restaurant without so much as tipping our compliant hostess (which was the norm at the time).

As we neared the turn of the century, a new millennium, we became aware of the Y2K scare. In contrast to the fears of a potential worldwide infrastructure outage, we Americans organized a fun scavenger hunt for a group of friends. New Year's Eve found us dispersed around the streets of our city looking for items to bring back and win the game. Nothing unusual happened after the midnight countdown, and our merriment continued. By the end of January, my brother Tim wed the girl he'd fallen in love with there in Hainan. My family put on a beautiful Christian wedding ceremony, while the bride's family provided the traditional Chinese banquet, making a long but happy day. The marriage of a missionary kid to a native of the island would be the first but not the last for my family.

By the end of that eventful year, I had accumulated a year's worth of college credits via a Stateside correspondence course program. But it didn't feel like enough in my newfound pursuit of a bachelor's degree. I felt a pull to leave China and start fresh as a full-time student in the United States. Restlessness stirred in my heart, pointing to a longing for a life change. I was twenty-three. Maybe it was just a part of growing up, wanting to plant my own roots somewhere, wanting what my siblings were finding in their life partners. Maybe it was wanting a fancy certificate many at my age had already achieved. The time would come for me to teach my final class, get back on the plane, say goodbye to a chapter—no, an era—of my life. Without ambitions of returning to China, that era would quietly slip away, entombed below the dust of time. It would not revive until I put fingers to keyboard almost two decades later, describing and exploring memories of that long-lost past.

Life in the States brought me face-to-face with yet another winding road full of choices and seeming delays. I do not know the extent of God's merciful protection over the next three and a half years in which I had yet to grow up, but I suspect it was much more than I deserved. With a good eye for his daughter's well-being; even with an ocean between us; my dad would gently encourage me to keep my eyes on Christ. The respect I had for him was the key to ultimately finding my way.

God's good favor providentially brought me to the completion of a four-year degree and getting hired in the one place I wanted to land: Southern California. Forgoing commencement ceremonies, I crossed the country to begin a new teaching position. My boss hoped I could commit to two years, but something held me back. By the start of that school year, I entered a new relationship in my personal life that would soon pivot me for a destiny I'd never have guessed. It was a plan only God could have orchestrated; a plan that would meet the longings of my heart.

17
That Unseen Hand

AFTER A SWIFT SWAT AND A STARTLED SQUEAL, A DEEP VOICE to my right proclaimed, "Welcome to the Air Force, Mrs. Dea!" That solemn glide beneath the honor guard's drawn sabers demonstrated a symbolic safe passage into marriage. I entered a completely new world clutching the hand of my second lieutenant. Family and friends who knew my history predicted I'd do well in this life. They said since I was used to traveling and moving, I'd manage better than others. But they never mentioned the military community. I knew almost nothing of it; never had the opportunity to enter in. I only saw the exterior—the flawless uniforms pressed and starched topped with a nice cover and polished shoes that pressed staunchly to the ground.

My husband had forewarned me about the hardships and sacrifices of being a military wife, offering an "out" before he proposed, in case the realities sounded too difficult, too much to process. He wanted me to decide if I'd rather be with someone who had a nine-to-five job that would allow me to settle down in one fixed location. As much as I could not fully encapsulate all he expressed about a life of service in the armed forces, none of what he said gave me pause to consider breaking up. He'd pursued me like no other and I'd fallen in love that first year in California. When he put a ring on my finger, tears gushed freely from what felt like a busted dam. At last, my turn had arrived. There was no doubt this was the life partner God had brought into my life. On top of that, I was proud to marry a man who had vowed to defend our constitution and protect our land. Brian was twice as handsome in uniform, an air of strength and loyalty about him. He was a humble leader I chose to follow.

With my father's blessing, I purposed to "do him good and not evil all the days of [my] life." I determined I'd be the kind of spouse whose husband could "safely trust in her, so that he [would] have no need of spoil." My aim was to pattern my role beside that quintessential wife described in Proverbs 31.

Though there have been struggles, difficulty, and frustrations in regard to military life, they pale in comparison to what I faced in my personal life. It began with seeking to grow our family long before my husband felt ready. I grew up with the singular belief that marriage was the avenue in which to bring children into the world. God designed it that way and he was the One who rewarded his people with "the fruit of the womb." Biological children were a gift and "heritage of the Lord." Watching my mother's belly grow large with my younger siblings arriving and expanding our home, I presumed that was the blueprint for any "normal" Christian couple. Adoption was great, but it was something for all "those other people" I couldn't identify with. Infertility was also a foreign concept I never grappled with until I found myself face-to-face with its ugly spores sucking the life out of my preconceived, albeit lifelong, notions.

God, in his unfathomable wisdom and understanding, knew this about me. He knew I would need to learn that as a woman it wasn't about measuring up to my mother or achieving that proverbial full quiver. Like the Old Testament story of Rachel, he understood it would take me a good, long season before and after giving birth to my firstborn son. As I wrestled with trying to loosen infertility's grip, God reminded me of a time in my teens when he had specifically set my heart aglow upon reading Isaiah's prophetic words to God's people. He had graciously given me a glimpse of his plan for my future. I went back to that moment of reading about sons and daughters coming from another place to be "nursed at thy side" (Isaiah 60:4). I may not have been pursuing my heavenly Father's will, but he was pursuing me to accomplish it.

My husband's heart was also softened to adoption. It was in the joys and heartaches of that season, God brought a man into my husband's work life. It was someone who had founded an organization to train and prepare Christian families for fostering and adopting. We soon learned of the deep love in the Father's heart toward the fatherless. In unison, our own hearts were set aflame with the burden and calling to step into fostering displaced children in our community.

It was just a matter of time before my husband and I became licensed foster parents at our second duty station. As a little boy, our son naturally stepped in, offering himself as an instant, built-in playmate to the children we took in. The new, satisfying role of being mother to not only my child but also a sibling set completely engulfed my life. But it was only a few short months that the Air Force took us in another direction, a direction back to my roots. It was during that overseas assignment in South Korea that the three of us were able to jump on a short flight over to Hong Kong. As much as we missed our foster daughters, hoping we had made a difference in their lives, a long-awaited dream of mine had come to pass at last. My heart was so ready for it.

It was the week of Thanksgiving, 2014, and I was delighted to be visiting parts of my childhood that had profoundly shaped me. Nostalgia came flooding in as we entered the Star Ferry Pier, the mode of transportation we chose to get to Hong Kong Island. All the old-fashioned bells and whistles of the pier were in place as usual, as though nothing had changed the past thirty years. We three walked straight into the ship's antiquated charm, my past submerged in Hong Kong's past.

Where had time gone? I mused. My redheaded son leaned an elbow over the ship's banister as we floated across the bay. I pulled my iPhone from my side pocket and snapped a few quick solo shots of him. Unlike me, he had no siblings clustered about him, sharing experiences. All my attention fixed on my son—the next generation standing where I had stood, continuing the story. Our beautiful boy was beginning to see and learn where part of his story began. I grabbed ahold of the banister as I felt the gentle pitch and roll of the ship beneath my feet. Together we gazed silently out toward the spectacular skyline, and my thoughts drifted back to my early childhood when I'd stood gazing over the same banister.

That familiar fishy smell tickled my nostrils. It was, after all, "Heung Gong," literally translated "fragrant harbor." Salt-laden air filled my lungs as I breathed slow and deep. The green murky water that slapped up to the docks was too cloudy to see past an inch or two from the surface. There was no telling what types of creatures swam below the surface. Taking the iconic double-ended, bottle-green-and-ivory Star Ferry across Victoria Harbor was one of my all-time favorite ways to travel, even if it was only eleven minutes per trip. It wasn't very often that my parents had taken us kids the slow way across the harbor. My dad usually drove us in our van, whizzing through the underground tunnel, white lights streaking past overhead.

Arriving at the pier meant slowing down and deliberately leaving the city's rush behind for a few moments. Even paying the surprisingly cheap fare of just a few coins brought us out of the spending frenzy within the city and took us back in time. A quiet calm surrounded us as we walked into the sleepy waiting section of the pier for the scheduled ferry to arrive. Chairs lined the walls. There were never many seats, but there were always enough.

The Star Ferry did not care to compete with any other mode of transportation. In fact, it seemed to defy any and all of it. The ferry line kept old Hong Kong alive. It offered a glimpse of what life used to be like before modern commerce swung into high gear. The Star Ferry was not a place to be reminded of the millions of things needing to get done. Flashy screens were not present there. Distractions with the entertainment world, media advertisements, and cares of the outside world were lost in the moment. Smartphones were only a futuristic dream in those days. Male passengers often carried a rolled newspaper under their arms. Most people simply resigned themselves to waiting idly, checking the clock on the wall for accurate time.

When the scheduled ship arrived, and it always arrived on schedule, anticipation would build in the waiting room. As though one unit, we passengers arose and moved toward a gated barrier. Bay breezes wafted throughout. Then the porter opened the gateway to allow entrance rounding the corner down toward the ramp. The confined entryway swallowed up the outpouring of passengers eager to climb aboard and set sail. One or two of the ship's crew, dressed in navy uniforms with white stripes on sailor-style lapels, prepared to toss heavy ropes to the dock and wind around iron bolts as wide as seats. The men skillfully maneuvered alongside the ship, the engine throttling as it inched closer until its hull bumped up against the dock, and brought the ferry to a secure hold. They worked in unison with the rhythm of the sea, as if they could do it all blindfolded.

The gangplank reached across to make a level, sturdy bridge between the ferry and the dock. Exiting passengers stood in mass, watching and waiting for the crew to provide access. Then, like a tidal wave, they thundered off the ship, surging up the walkway at an even pace toward land. They were gone in a flash, and the empty bridge beckoned new passengers to come aboard. As a unit, we proceeded purposefully to get onboard. There was no turning back! Even if we wanted to stop and observe the scene, the movement of people in motion with the wide-awake undercurrent thrust all passengers forward as the ferry gently rocked and reeled. It was as though an unseen hand pushed us along and over onto the boat's lower deck.

I always wanted to move over to the opposite side of the ship to get an open-air sea-level view of the spectacular harbor named after the lovely Queen Victoria. If it was cold or rainy, we made our way upstairs to sit on the varnished, unpadded wood benches. Closed windows kept the chill out. The unglamorous, hollow interior steered clear of the rest of Hong Kong's luxury, faithfully maneuvering passengers back and forth from one skyline to the next. I liked it best on a warm, sunny day below, leaning against the banister, simply admiring glistening waters as they buoyantly lapped their strength against an unobstructed panorama.

The putter of the engine would rev up, and out onto the postcard-perfect-looking bay we would float, nice and easy, breaking away from the constraints of the pier. I loved the taste of warm, salty air as the ferry increased in speed, the rush of wind smoothing the day's concerns from my brow. The water slapped against the hull as the ship expertly rode the waves, charging ahead with unfettered exuberance. I rather enjoyed the "rocking horse" effect on board. The lurching of the water was a powerful force beneath me. The current constantly swished and threatened to knock me off my feet if I didn't walk with the sway of the boat.

Like the forward motion of the ship, the unseen hand of God ever propelled me onward. The current of my life continuously switched directions, trying as it might to knock me down and swallow me up. My worldview expanded at such a young age, sealing permanent memories that would connect to future events God had in store. The door to my world thrust open so far and wide, allowing me a real and personal taste of life on opposite sides of the planet. Who would have thought an ordinary girl like me would be given such a gift? I still wonder why I was chosen among so few. Did I walk through each passageway well? Like a blank canvas, my mind worked in overdrive, processing sketches of the world around me.

I wore the "missionary kid" label as though it were stitched onto my blouse or sleeve. There was no way to hide it or pretend I was someone else. All my travels and adventures shaped me, tried to define me, but ultimately, I was more than that. Maneuvering away from the first part of my life only to enter the next major part did not end the formative work God had begun in me.

With all the uprooting, transplanting, and grafting in to new communities, my biggest question remains. *Who does God say I am?* Out of all the good things we can do or be here in this life, which is most important or precious to him? What is most valued in his sight? He sees much deeper than my current role or list of roles I've lived out. There will be no rank, label, or badge to hold out to him when I stand before his throne one day. The concern is whether heaven is my final destination, whether my name is found etched in his book.

At the end of the day, just as Esther stood alone before her king, devoid of self, my concern is also acceptance and belonging. My King's view of me, his judgment of me, is most important. How he sees me—beyond the long list of descriptions that identify me in this world—must be where I plant my value and worth. Because Jesus Christ is my Lord and Savior, I know that I am his. I'm beloved in his sight. I'm redeemed by his atoning blood once shed on the cross for me. I'm clothed in his righteousness. I'm a child of God. That moment my youthful conscience became aware, he began drawing me to himself, and thereafter I came seeking, asking, knocking. Though I've often lived selfishly and foolishly, distancing myself from God, I'm thankful for his prodding to repent and return to him. He will always be the solid Rock upon which I stand.

My heavenly Father gives value to the assorted pieces of life. None of it is random. He shows how to live effectively in the current picture because of the former. Though the apostle Paul wrote about forgetting and letting go of "those things which are behind" in order to reach toward what lies before (Philippians 3:13), he also testified boldly of his own history that led him to Christ. Because the King of Kings is everlasting; is not limited by time, disruption, or anything else; my identifying roles simply come and go while my place of belonging remains in his loving hands.

18
I'm Home

Present Day

I LISTENED UNCOMFORTABLY AS MY HUSBAND OF EIGHTEEN years began to tell me things I never wanted to entertain. He talked about the reality that God may choose not to heal him of the disease that had savagely permeated his lymphatic system for a full year. He had received great medical care and treatment but was feeling familiar side effects all over again that had brought him into an acute awareness that perhaps this was a tell-tale sign signaling the end of his time here on earth, that it was no longer about beating cancer but rather being prepared for eternity and letting go of all he held dear.

While the phrase "till death do us part" bears no relevance in the eternal security of the redeemed child of God, it does tend to hold some weight for any serious couple facing one another at the wedding altar. When I reverently voiced those words to my husband along with "in sickness and in health," he and I were two young and healthy individuals with zero concern of any sort of health crisis. Eighteen years together and we were still stewarding our lives well and staying active physically. We had yet to reach the halfway point in our life together—a completely assumed projection.

Ever since childhood, I'd learned to treasure people and places while also holding them loosely. A rotating door brought them in and out of my life, but family remained. Quiet conversations after a year of traversing through what was supposed to be a very treatable type of cancer left me with a sickening pit in my stomach. I had to acknowledge the fact that sometimes God's answer is indeed no. Sometimes the closest family member dies too early and those remaining have to move on and discover what good plans God has yet for them to fulfill.

I had never seen my husband at such a low point. He was known for his uber-positive attitude, his call sign of many years being "Sunny" Dea. I was the loyal military wife, the cheering partner through every rank, promotion, accolade, throughout his entire career. But once more, I remembered to whom I ultimately belonged in both this life and the life thereafter. In unabashed prayerful wrestling, Jesus whispered my name, *Faith. Remember your namesake as I've defined it and you.* I knew his voice; the voice of Truth. I leaned in.

My whole life was about absorbing faith—a good, steady one passed down from my parents. All my life I'd reaped the benefit from my spiritual inheritance, journeying on a faith walk with consistent family members at my side. Could I trust my Lord alone? This turbulent storm refused to relent, trying as it might to grab ahold of my sail and vector me elsewhere, away from resting in Christ. The unknown future brewed chilling thoughts and fears based entirely on what could become reality, not on what actually was real and true. Loss and grief had shown up before in my marriage, but I understood this would be the greatest loss of all.

On the afternoon of August 14, 2023, just a few weeks after my husband had expressed his concern about the future, I heaved great sobs onto his shoulder. A floodgate had opened and I let the tears pour out and wash over the both of us. But on that day, those were not troubled tears of grief. No, they were tears of relief and joy. We'd received confirmation that Brian was in complete remission. God had moved in favor of our fervent prayers and all those who had rallied around us to intercede on behalf of our family, Jesus himself doing so at the right hand of the Father (Romans 8:34). Our petition for healing and life was granted, and gratitude spilled forth.

In his goodness and mercy, my heavenly Father reminded me very poignantly that it is he who promises to journey through life with me, unseen with human eyes but not with human faith. My seat of security is found in him. He is not an off-and-on God, present only at times depending on his interest or my behavior. Jesus Christ is sovereign over every detail, every cell in our bodies, every shift in circumstance and season. My job is to abide in him first and foremost. No matter the altered course, nothing can change that.

One Month Later

I COULDN'T STOP SHIVERING. WITH CHILLED FINGERS, I clasped both sides of my jacket zipper at the bottom to zip it all the way up to my neck. As I looked down to my toes, I wished I'd worn something other than the open toe sandals. My feet were wet and cold. It was only in the mid-fifties Fahrenheit, not enough to be that bad, but we'd had such nice, summer weather my body hadn't time to adjust to this much of a dip in temperature. I thought if my feet were covered in warm shoes, I probably wouldn't be shaking like I was. I hoped it wasn't noticeable, but realized if it was, I had every reason to shake on a day like this.

I breathed deep, letting out a slow exhale. I was cold, but not freezing. My right side was getting wet from a light rain blowing south, and I stood just under the shelter of the pavilion. The woman who stood beside me to my left allowed her mourning tears to fall silently. She sniffed and dabbed at her face with a white tissue, placing it back into her uniform pocket. Another woman behind me was also crying gently. I knew both of them by name. At events in the past, we'd shared laughter and lighthearted conversations. Today, the gloomy weather seemed to prod at the tears to fall as easily as the steady drizzle that morning.

I glanced over at my husband who stood tall and handsome in his dress-blue uniform. His soft peaked service cap stretched wide and snug over his head, covering all signs he was bald. He was mentally preparing his speech he would give momentarily. The poly wool fabric blend served him and the others well in this weather. Formal and proper, all other active-duty members wore the same pressed Air Force blue dress uniform. I felt bad for my friend next to me in a skirt. She could have worn the trousers, knowing how the weather looked that day, but she wore a skirt instead, bare legs exposed. I didn't notice any quivering in spite of it.

Why am I still shivering? Lord, I need you to help me relax. I wanted to appear calm. It wasn't that I was emotionally troubled. I was not distraught or deeply grieving for the one for whom we'd all gathered. I'd never personally met him. It's just that I was not ready to feel this cold. I decided at the next break in the service that I'd quietly open my wide umbrella. It would shield me from the wind that was continuing to blow moisture in my direction as well as on those congregating beside me. When the moment came, I pressed the button and eased the canopy ribs forward till they clicked secure, then lowered the bar to rest in the crook of my arm, balancing it with my left hand at the handle. It helped immensely.

Brian and I had decided weeks ago that we would travel home a day early from vacation so that we could be at the memorial service. A letter I'd received from the deceased member's parents spoke of how they looked forward to seeing my husband and I that day. We were moved by the tenderness and graciousness of the grieving father and mother. The letter reminded us we ought to be present. Brian reflected that this is how we want to live our lives—not for and about ourselves, but for others. I agreed.

We stood solemnly, gathered together under the small pavilion. Family members and a few close friends sat stiffly on metal benches. We had all taken out the same part of our day for a young officer now gone, for his family who remained a part of us. Smart phones were silenced, perhaps even forgotten for the time being. Personal problems and worries set aside. An annoying low tire pressure light had flicked on in my car just as I drove up to the cemetery. As usual, with any maintenance light that illuminates on my instrumental panel, my internal stress hormone peaks. When the service began, that was no longer important. All cares could wait. It felt as though each in attendance resigned to stay planted in their spot, respectfully unwavering from start to finish.

At the close of the service, the motion was given to ceremoniously greet the family. It was a gradual break away from fixed positions, arms extending for handshakes, words of sympathy spoken softly. Others moved in for heartfelt hugs, pausing to share fond memories. Feet slowly shuffled toward the front of the pavilion. Those in civilian clothes were fewer in number than those in military uniform. The active-duty members presented a warm tide of blue in contrast to bleaker colors worn for the day. My husband blended in easily, coordinating attire and a strong camaraderie doing the trick.

Long ago, when I was a new military wife, I was so nervous, unable to see past the uniform, intimidated by the awe of those who served all around me. I entered my new community feeling much like a foreigner. Rank had been unknown and unfamiliar back then. I remember Brian explaining the difference between enlisted and officer ranks, and it took me some time to remember the sequence for each. From my view, they all looked good across the board. The exterior served as a barrier, blinding me to the character of the men and women behind the dress code. I couldn't relate personally apart from those whom I knew to be brothers and sisters in Christ. My ministry past didn't bridge over to my secular present, I mistakenly thought. Somewhere along the line, I needed to figure out how the two were linked.

I closed my umbrella tightly, calmed by the chance at last to move toward the sweet mother whose thin arms gripped the triangularly folded flag. A warm feeling had surged, overcoming my initial shivering state.

It felt so right and natural to be there. My upbringing had shaped me to adapt at each spot on the map I identified as home. Home came wrapped in all the flavors, the types and assortment of people that made up each place. I'd been ushered into the spouse position, young and naïve as I was. Though life experiences showed me life itself was fragile and could change at a moment's notice, I was no longer a fish out of water. My ability to support those around us was sharpened and effective, reminding me that it was never about finding myself, but instead, seeing how I fit in the magnificent kingdom work here on earth.

Epilogue

Today I'm thankful that I've been able to put meaning and hopefully some depth to many of my memories and most recent experiences unraveled here. My aim has been to disentangle each one, combing through with "the wisdom that is from above" (James 3:17).

I would be remiss to leave out stories of some who came to know the Lord by way of my family's ministry in China. It's a ministry that has extended its reach to this present day. Redemptive threads weaved through time and place have continued to connect the Baucums to the people of Hong Kong and many throughout China. I pray you'll be blessed reading each of the brief testimonies below. Like me, these friends trod winding paths that led them to a secure and unfailing dwelling place found only in Christ.

Cedric's Story

While my sisters and I were befriending the daughters of the Mercedes owner who lived next door, my older brothers were getting to know some boys around Fairview Park's sprawling neighborhood. One of note was a kid named

Cedric. Ross and Tim intersected with Cedric off and on, noticing him out and about, often in the middle of petty arguments with other youth. Cedric was rough and rebellious, yet he had a magnetic personality and was also a natural leader. My brothers had no idea local triad gangs were actively trying to recruit him.

My brothers soon invited him over to our home and then church. They found out Cedric was from a nice family that was exceptionally welcoming and gracious. They were even faithful members at a Lutheran church. Cedric's dad played the organ for the services. But Cedric did not have an interest in Christianity; he did not see any utility in going to church with his parents.

God was at work nonetheless, both at that point in time as well as long before the Baucums and the Wongs "coincidentally" ended up on the same neighborhood block. Cedric just so happened to be the great-grandson of one of the faithful members of that historical Swatow Baptist Church. His grandmother had been saved and baptized and did what she could to serve her community in the 1940s. Generations followed suit. Cedric came along but was one of a kind. Religion was dull and unappealing to him. But there was something about those Baucum boys that caused him to agree to go to church with them. There was something about Butterfly Bay Baptist Church that piqued his interest. Before he turned eighteen, Cedric got saved and baptized and surrendered his life to preach the gospel.

Candy's Story

Candy and Cedric met at Butterfly Bay Baptist Church, and my dad married them in 1999. But her story did not start there.

It began with the Catholic church, though no one in her family was Catholic. Her parents sent her to a local Catholic school because it provided a quality education. The Roman Catholic Church had established a respectable presence in Hong Kong. A missionary district had been set up long before. Both Catholic and Protestant churches had created a partnership with the colonial government for the provision of education in Hong Kong. Many of their institutions were subsidized by the Hong Kong government and maintained religious sponsoring bodies.

Candy enjoyed her school, beginning in kindergarten. She went to Mass when she was in elementary grades, but remembers only being interested in playing with her friends. She does not remember any gospel message, even though the crucifix prominently hung on display.

For secondary level (high school), Candy was placed in a Christian school. It was all based on her grades and finding the right fit. Again, there was no religious preference on the part of her parents. They just wanted her to get a good education, and the government's educational system made that possible. At this point in her life, Candy understood the basic difference between religions. She did not identify herself with any religious belief. Rather, she would confidently tell people that she only believed in herself.

But God was at work in Candy's world. A teacher at her new Christian school invited her to an evangelistic revival meeting. The gospel was presented clearly. She was counseled after the service and decided right then to believe in Jesus, receiving him as her personal Savior. After that, she asked her teacher lots of questions and why there was only one true God. The Holy Spirit began to give Candy a perception she had not had before. She was still regularly attending Mass with people she'd grown up with, but all of a sudden, she did not believe it was necessary to go to confession or perform the rituals. Her teacher said she was biblically correct in not having to go through a priest in order to be in right standing with God. Candy understood there was a relationship piece missing in Catholicism. Following her teacher's encouragement, she decided it was time to say goodbye to the church community she had belonged to for many years. It was not easy, but she did it.

Once Candy left the Catholic Church, she and two classmates decided to search for a Christian church. Attending her teacher's place of worship wasn't convenient since she lived too far away. After school one day, while the girls were still in uniform, they wandered around Butterfly Bay Estate, the neighborhood next to where Candy lived. "Not all who wander are lost" could be said of these girls in that moment! A few windows were opened in the community center that day, and they could hear a guitar strumming and voices singing along. Like butterflies to open flowers, the girls were drawn to the pleasant music inside. They found Luke and another young man who told them this was in fact a Christian church and they were welcome to come back for the Sunday service. It was 1988. The girls had coincidently discovered the newly established Butterfly Bay Baptist Church.

Candy and her friends attended service that Sunday and every Sunday thereafter. She believes it wasn't coincidence that led her to that particular church. The Spirit of God was at work in leading and illuminating her path as she chose to trust and follow Jesus Christ. She is also grateful for her Christian teacher's influence to pursue truth.

Polly's Story

As a teenager, Polly attended a Christian high school, not because she or her parents were Christians, but because it was simply a good school. Polly believes the school's Christian influence planted good seed in her heart. One day a classmate invited her to visit a church called Kin Sang Baptist. Neither Polly nor her classmate were believers yet, but they were both curious and open to learning more about the Christ they'd been exposed to. Nothing held Polly back from going. She wasn't sure what to expect at this particular church, but she was willing and ready to find out.

The two girls showed up on Sunday morning and were ushered down the hall to the small meeting area. The church operated during the week as a child care facility and preschool. Brightly colored decals plastered the walls and clung to the windows. Children's art decorated the large bulletin boards along with notices for parents. Even the boys' and girls' restrooms had mini toilets and sinks for the little children.

When the meeting room doors opened, Polly was surprised to see a mixture of Chinese people and foreigners. There were only a few in attendance, but they happily sang a special welcome song for Polly and her friend. That alone made a big impression on the newcomers. From that day on, Polly attended regularly. Something about the playfully decorated walls, the atmosphere, and the gathering of strangers acknowledging her worth had collectively grasped her attention, and she wanted to hold still and take in more.

Questions arose in her heart and mind. Questions about what Christianity was really all about. Questions about the reality of Christ and why she needed Him. Questions that went as far back to when she was a small child seeing her grandfather lying still in his coffin, wondering where he went. Fear and sadness had plagued her young heart upon seeing her dad cry that day. She knew her grandpa would not be waking up. Worry crept in, telling her she might lose her parents in the same manner. She did not understand death, yet it stirred deep questions and emotions. Outside, she would find comfort looking up at the big blue sky. Polly believed that there must be a Creator who controlled everything. She knew instinctively the small statues her parents purchased at the market couldn't possibly be gods deserving of worship. The glazed, miniature faces only created fear and unrest.

Polly battled the universal "work of the law written in their hearts, their conscience also bearing witness, and their thoughts..." (Romans 2:15). And like the scripture says so perfectly, "Because that which may be known of God is manifest in them: for God hath shewed it unto them. For the invisible things of him from the creation of the world are clearly seen, being understood by the things that are made, even his eternal power and Godhead; so that they are without excuse" (Romans 1:19–20).

About one year after showing up at church on a Wednesday night, Pastor Baucum, my dad, closed out a sermon in his usual manner, inviting anyone who wasn't sure of their salvation to accept Christ. Polly was ready. She raised her hand and subsequently received Jesus as her personal Lord and Savior.

Today, Polly is married to a Christian man she met at the same church where she got saved. He too came to Christ through that ministry. Together they are raising a beautiful daughter, teaching and showing her real truth and love that casts out fear.

Peggy's Story

OUT OF ALL THE MANY MAINLAND CHINESE WHO INTERSECTed with our family, one was a young wife who, unbeknownst to her, carried a Christian heritage from her mother's family that had all but died off. Peggy came into our lives interested in learning English. My mom developed a friendship with her and slowly guided the English conversations toward the English Scriptures. Peggy was not a believer but remembered that her own grandparents had been of the same faith as ours.

Years later Peggy would share how her grandparents were the first in her family whose lives were changed by the ministry of American missionaries in China. Her mother's parents had been hired servants of missionaries who had come to live and serve a poor community in Henan province. At the time, her grandparents were raising six children. The missionaries helped care for the young family and even provided financial assistance to Peggy's mother and some of the siblings to pursue higher education.

Peggy was raised by her grandparents, who modeled Christian character. Her first formative years were shaped by two people who did their best to quietly and wisely live out their faith in Christ under tight government control after Chairman Mao came into power. They remained faithful and secretly held Bible studies and worship in their home.

With the fear of arrest, labor camps, and even execution during the tumultuous Cultural Revolution of the 1960s and '70s, most of Peggy's aunts and uncles abandoned their own faith in God. They, along with their children, including Peggy, adhered to the communist indoctrination and heavy propaganda over the course of their lives in China. There wasn't much opportunity outside of working under or alongside the scrutiny of the Chinese Communist Party. Her grandparents did not try to persuade or control their kids. They just prayed for them.

After Peggy got married in 1997, she and her husband

moved to Hainan Island. Peggy decided to enroll in a language school to improve her English. Coincidentally, that same language school employed three American teachers. All three teachers were in one family and were also undercover missionaries.

It wasn't long before Peggy was invited to learn more at her American teacher's house. A friendly relationship developed, and she was introduced to the teachings of the Bible. It was there that she witnessed Christian character modeled in our home. That alone impressed her more than what we were trying to teach or say. She came to realize it was a reflection of the essence she had witnessed in her grandparents' lives years ago. God was at work in Peggy's life even before she put the pieces together and came to understand what He was doing. The prayers of her faithful grandparents had not gone unheeded at heaven's gates.

Today, Peggy and her family live in California. For almost two decades, they have been faithfully involved members of their local church. They have each come to put their faith and trust in Jesus Christ, to grow together in the Word, and to enjoy the blessings of a Christ-centered home. What was once a fading heritage of faith became a reignited legacy connected by Truth from one generation to the next.

John's Story (in his own words)

I WAS WANDERING. I FELT HOPELESS IN SPIRIT AND MEANINGless in life. While I was teaching English in a foreign language school, I got to know the Baucum family and found they were different. They always showed kindness and concern for people. They were always energized in every ordinary and tiny duty. I was amazed at their attitude to their obligation and devotion to their responsibilities.

I wondered what made them so different. Was it only because they were from a different country and background? I searched for a satisfying answer and discovered they were Christians. I admired their attitude and way of life.

Mr. Baucum graciously offered me the opportunity to tutor their children in math. This gave me many opportunities to communicate with his family.

I didn't like the boss of the foreign language school where Mr. Baucum and I taught. On one occasion I asked Mr. Baucum, "Why are you so devotedly working for such a school with no future?" He told me he had his reasons. I wondered what those reasons were.

Mr. Baucum provided me many Christian books and a Bible. This was something I had longed for since my college days because at the time there were no Bibles for sale in China's bookstores.

I began to search out the Bible stories I had heard during my college years. I had majored in English language and literature, so I read biblical stories about the flood, Noah, Abraham, Moses, and David.

When I came to the story about the cross of Christ, I didn't understand. Mr. Baucum explained to me why Christ was crucified. I thought a lot about it. It was during a Sunday service in his home that Mr. Baucum preached that Christ was crucified, not because *he* did wrong but because *we* did wrong; all of us had sinned against God. He died on the cross in our place so that we might be forgiven and live forever.

When I meditated on Romans 5:8, which says, "But God commendeth his love toward us, in that, while we were yet sinners, Christ died for us," I was amazed that the love of

God was poured out by the Holy Spirit into my heart. I was literally brought back to the scene of the cross and heard Christ crying, "Father, forgive them, for they know not what they do" (Luke 23:34). For the first time, I comprehended the love of God and the forgiveness found in Christ. I bowed to thank God for his love on the cross and praised him for this great salvation. The word of God came alive to me. I found fulfillment and satisfaction in the salvation in Christ which is presented in the word of God.

I found meaning and energy to live with God and for God. He healed my brokenness as well as broken relationships with others. I began to reconcile with the people I had hurt and with those who had hurt me. I shared the good tidings with them earnestly. God greatly blessed my family, and my wife got saved. Together we began to share a new life message. I was convinced that the only meaningful life is to share the gospel of Christ. I committed myself to do this, and God has faithfully led me forward.

I translated for Mr. Baucum on Sunday while he taught me the Word during the week. I was also able to study Bible lessons from Bob Jones University material. Mr. Baucum set a good example for me to follow. I was ordained in November 2004. I have served in ministry since then. My family and I have been greatly blessed all these years, and I often recall the words of David in Psalm 23:1–3:

> The Lord is my shepherd; I shall not want.
>
> He maketh me to lie down in green pastures,; he leadeth me beside the still waters.
>
> He restoreth my soul: he leadeth me in the paths of righteousness for his name's sake.

Each of these individuals represents a narrow fraction of an extensive number of people I could have reached out to. I'm grateful they each willingly and readily shared their testimonies without any coercion or lengthy forethought. While I was glad to be a part of the intricate network that led so many Chinese friends to Christ, I took for granted their backstories. However, their faithfulness began to intrigue me as I explored the ways God was at work in a place that greatly impacted my life. These few I've listed above have been a part of my story for more than thirty years. Their lives have influenced me more than I can express in this paragraph. It has been one of my greatest gifts simply to be one small part of the family and church God used to usher in their eternal salvation. My aim here is to showcase the goodness and glory of our Lord and Savior Jesus Christ.

Endnotes

1   This Cantonese documentary is available on the Swatow Baptist Church of Kowloon City Facebook page at https://www.facebook.com/SBCKC under the Videos tab (https://www.facebook.com/watch/?v=345000536270947&ref=sharing).

2   "Kai Tak Airport History," Gwulo.com, info submitted May 1, 2008, https://gwulo.com/kai-tak-airport-history.

3   Hugh Farmer, "Kai Tak Airport – 1925 to 1945, A Brief History," The Industrial History of Hong Kong Group, industrialhistoryhk.org, October 15, 2017, https://industrialhistoryhk.org/kai-tak-airport-1925-1945-brief-history/.

4   Christopher DeWolf, "The Hong Kong Airport Story: Then, Now and the Future," CathayPacific.com, July 19, 2019, https://www.cathaypacific.com/cx/en_HK/inspiration/hong-kong/hong-kong-airport-story-now-future.html.

5   Marilyn R. Gardner, Between Worlds: Essays on Culture and Belonging (n.p.: Doorlight Publications, 2014), 144–48.

Acknowledgments

DAD, EVER SINCE YOU NOTICED AND RAVED ABOUT THAT FIRST, heartfelt "poem" I wrote on your desktop in Hainan, I've craved and valued your attention like no other. Your fatherly praise was the spark I needed to know that what I expressed in the written word meant something deep to someone other than myself. Mom, your continual interest in reading everything I write, encouraging me along the way, spurs me on in this writing life.

To my husband. Simply knowing that I enjoy writing has been enough reason for you to prod me forward no matter the financial cost. Thank you, Brian, for putting things into perspective for me when I voiced my hesitancy, my doubts, or my indecision. Thank you for moving the 2020 Christian Writer's Market Guide, sitting in "saved for later" on Amazon.com into check out. That book led me to eventually hiring my first editor and coach, Alice Crider.

Alice, I am so grateful you do what you do for Christian writers. You patiently and loyally coached me through a plan to get my work out of the "non-commercially viable" category. Your line edits awoke an attune attention to detail I thought I had, but severely lacked. Thank you for your honest praise and solid feedback after each revised chapter.

I owe a debt of thanks to my copy editor, Deb Hall, who helped me clarify thoughts and include many extra final details including this Acknowledgment section. As with you and all the support I've received, God's providence is most definitely what got us connected.

To Rachel Waldock, Rachel Miller, Alisha Coffey, and Mindy Black. Thank you, friends, for offering much needed feedback. The message of this story would not be near as deep or true to myself without each of your insights given.

Swatow Baptist Church of Kowloon City put together an excellent documentary detailing the history of their church and graciously posted it to their Facebook page for all to enjoy. The granddaughter of one of the founding members shared it with me. Thank you, Li Mai Lai, for cherishing your own history, and receiving all my questions. Without you, this book would not have the introductory setting which perfectly set the stage for my family's entrance into Hong Kong. Thank you, Rebecca and Charity, for translating.

Many thanks to the following ladies that took the time to read and write thoughtful endorsements: Dr. Heather Daveduik Gingrich, Dr. Joy Angela, Gayle Tomlinson, Cathy Hall, and Michelle Elaine Burton. Each of these women are incredibly accomplished, and actively serve in their fields of ministry. I am humbled by the fact that they would validate my work.

My brother Tim. You reminded me that this is my story, through my own eyes. As a reader, you wanted to hear about me, not everyone else and all the ministries I originally went on and on about. I guess I needed permission to keep the narrative centered there. Thank you.

About the Author

FAITH CURRENTLY LIVES IN THE UNITED STATES WITH HER husband and three children; the eldest by birth, the younger two by adoption. She helps her family plant roots as quickly as possible at each duty station. The decision to live on base housing, rent, or purchase in town is always pressing long before orders arrive. The question of where to retire remains elusive.

Unraveled began on an old lap top after adopting and moving to Alabama in 2018. Faith was greatly impressed to write on the themes in this book. She continued after transferring to California, then published in Colorado. This heart of this book traveled with the author just like its story unfolded across continents.

Short, reflective moments of Faith's present-day life are found on her blog. Faith also writes devotionals for *Thrive,* a women's ministry that exists to refresh and partner with women ministering globally for the kingdom of God. She is active in her military community as well as in her local church. She currently homeschools her children. Writing nourishes her soul as well as being outdoors on warm, sunny days under the expanse of a deep, blue sky. She loves reading memoir but also Christian historical fiction. Gardening is a favorite hobby as well. Her greatest green-thumb success was growing and harvesting large batches of garlic in California. For not being a huge pet lover, particularly types that shed, she took in a two-year-old lab/husky mix. The dog needed a home, and the kids needed a furry friend.

Time with parents, siblings, and cousins is invaluable, and not often enough. Faith helps plan family reunions for the Baucum side. It is a serious undertaking for a large, growing family. A godly heritage is a priceless gift passed down from one generation to the next. It is one this book is meant to transmit.

Connect with Faith

http://faith2dea.blogspot.com
bestdeaever@gmail.com
https://www.facebook.com/faith.baucumdea
https://www.instagram.com/faithdea

Made in the USA
Middletown, DE
21 October 2024